A Royal British Columbia Museum Heritage Record

RESPONDING TO FASHION
The Clothing of the O'Reilly Family

Virginia A.S. Careless

ROYAL
BRITISH
COLUMBIA
MUSEUM

Province of British Columbia
Ministry of Tourism and
Ministry Responsible for Culture

Published by the Royal British Columbia Museum,
675 Belleville Street, Victoria, British Columbia, V8V 1X4, Canada.

Printed in Canada.

Canadian Cataloguing in Publication Data
Careless, Virginia.
    Responding to fashion

    (Heritage record, ISSN 0701-9556)

    ISBN 0-7718-9241-1

    1. O'Reilly, Charlotte Kathleen, 1867-1945 -
Clothing. 2. Clothing and dress - British Columbia
- Victoria - History. 3. O'Reilly Family - Museums
- British Columbia - Victoria. 4. Pt. Ellice House
(Victoria, B.C.) I. Royal British Columbia Museum.
II. Title. III. Series.

GT621.V53C37 1992   391'.009711'28   C92-092254-6

TABLE OF CONTENTS

I   INTRODUCTION

This project was based upon the collection of O'Reilly clothing at the Royal British Columbia Museum. The O'Reillys were an important family in this province and in Victoria in particular. Peter O'Reilly came to Victoria from Ireland in 1859 and in 1863 married Caroline A. Trutch, the sister of Joseph Trutch who became B.C.'s first Lieutenant-Governor. Peter worked as Stipendiary Magistrate, Gold Commissioner, and Indian Reserve Commissioner. In late 1867, the family moved into a house at Point Ellice in Victoria. This home remained in O'Reilly hands until 1975 when, then a private museum, it was purchased by the provincial government. We are fortunate that a massive collection of documents and artifacts that recorded much of B.C.'s history as well as their own, was saved by the O'Reillys over the years.

The Royal British Columbia Museum (RBCM) houses a part of their collection, mostly in the form of clothing, which itself comprises a sizeable section of our Clothing and Textile holdings. I was given the task of studying this clothing, especially that of the daughter of the family, Charlotte Kathleen (1867-1945). (See Appendix for family tree, and various Figures for photographs of Kathleen.) I was to focus on the alterations to the pieces that we have, as it was thought that these would be a good indicator of the family's financial situation, which we know changed drastically over the years.[1] It was expected that more clothes with alterations would be found corresponding to those times when money was scarce and new clothes could not be afforded.

Work began in the Summer of 1987 in conjunction with another project on the cooking activities of the same family. This first part of the report is followed by a second part on the O'Reillys' food: *Clue to a Culture: Food Preparation of the O'Reilly Family*. Although each part can stand alone, they are being presented together to obviate repeating introductory information in the second part.

It is necessary to begin by discussing the places where I did my research and the types of sources that I consulted. It will become apparent, as this report proceeds, how much the nature and organization of each collection of information affected my findings and the rate of progress and success in this project. My research revealed a great deal about the condition and accessibility of the information on the topic as well as about the topic itself. Accordingly, I will discuss my findings in both these areas. At the end of the report, I will look at the uses to which the findings have already been put, and other potential outlets that exist for them.

II   REPOSITORIES CONSULTED

1.   Point Ellice House

I was fortunate to have my work at Point Ellice House—home of the O'Reilly family—greatly facilitated by the staff of Heritage Conservation, now the Heritage Properties Branch, who provided me with ready access to the site and its collections. I was permitted to borrow certain items, the loan of which allowed me to study them in conjunction with our own collection. In return, I was able to contribute by giving tours of the house, training Branch guides, and consulting on their orientation videotapes as well as kitchen and Christmas programmes.

Pt. Ellice houses a wealth of material of various kinds. There are the three-dimensional ones such as furniture and other furnishings, clothing and textiles, needlework, sports equipment, housewares, carriages, travel souvenirs, medical and cooking supplies, and so forth. It also contains various two-dimensional documentary sources: prints and paintings, many done by family members; photographs, both unmounted and in frames; some diaries, letters, notebooks and address books; accounts and bills; house inventories; programmes for dances, concerts and regattas; invitations; calling cards; books of various kinds including text books; school exercise books; magazines and journals; and music, libretti, etc. The collection covers the life of the O'Reilly family, who were involved with the history of B.C. from the 1850s, and who occupied Pt. Ellice House from 1867 until its sale in 1976 to the Province of B.C. as a historic site.

The wealth of material at Pt. Ellice was rendered less accessible by a wealth of another sort: pests. In the course of studying the clothing, which had probably not been disturbed since the retirement of Curator Michael Zarb in February 1987, I found that moths were doing extensive and serious damage. Some pieces were covered with a fine sawdust-like powder of moth droppings; moving the piece would have virtually destroyed it when the crumbled surface was dislodged. The temporary staff at the house was planning to use mothballs as a remedy. On being asked about this procedure, I suggested that they contact Colleen Wilson, clothing and textile conservator at the RBCM, who would likely recommend freezing the pieces. She was consulted, and duly seconded to supervise the project, Operation Moth, for six months. The whole collection was completely examined, the displays disassembled, the affected artifacts bagged in plastic and taken off-site for freezing, and the house thoroughly cleaned.[2] Terrible things might have happened to the site had the moths stayed untreated.

The clean-up to some extent dealt with another pest—rats—whose leavings were soiling and damaging artifacts and, more seriously, whose chewing was destroying the collection. One book that I consulted, for example, was much less useful as a source than it should have been—its date had been eaten off. The rats posed a threat to the house's very existence, as it could all go up in flames were they to chew through the wiring. Rotting rat bodies (contrary to the ratman's asseveration, dead rats *do* smell) and concern about surprising living specimens (a staff member was bitten and needed rabies shots) impeded the process of research somewhat. Nevertheless, I was still able to examine the clothing and textiles at Pt. Ellice in a preliminary fashion before they were removed. As that part of the collection had not been returned to the site or unpacked at the time of writing this report, study of it in the light of subsequent documentary research was not possible.

The main area of concern in this project was the O'Reilly pieces in the RBCM, but those at Pt. Ellice were also useful in helping to fill out the total picture of the family's clothing. A drawback in relying too heavily on the Pt. Ellice collection is that the present Mrs. O'Reilly is a collector of clothing, and various pieces of hers were included in the artifacts that were purchased by the Government and left in the house.[3] Work is being done there to upgrade the cataloguing and in particular to clear up such ambiguities concerning the collection's provenance. But at the time of this study, one could not always be certain that an object there came from the family prior to John O'Reilly's marriage, unless there was documentation to establish it as such. Our collection is different in that it came, via the B.C. Archives and Records, from John's mother, or from John himself just after her death. Thus, we can be more easily convinced of the provenance.

Besides clothing, I looked at many of the other items listed above, in order to understand the human context in which the clothing existed, the accessories with which it was worn, and the activities with which it was associated. I studied the needlework in particular, both plain and fancy, to get a sense of the type of sewing done, and the colours and designs favoured. For similar reasons, I looked at the family paintings, and also the garden. In this latter work I was greatly assisted by Cyril Hume, period landscape consultant, who has been restoring the Pt. Ellice House garden. His findings were also of direct help in my cooking research.

I expected the photographs to be of special importance, as here one could see the clothing being worn and by whom, hair styles, jewellery, flowers, clothing accessories, and frequently other people and settings (if the location were not in a studio). Studio portraits are informative too, as the name of the photographer, often with his address, helps in establishing a date for the photo, and therefore for the clothing shown. As the previous curator at Pt. Ellice, Michael Zarb compiled a biographical file on the family that included the dates and destinations of their travel, such photographs can often be dated quite easily.[4] Thanks to photographs I was able to identify some clothing in the Royal B.C. Museum collection and, significantly, pieces which until then were not known to be O'Reilly ones; specific examples will be discussed later in this report. I also found that a great many of the clothes thus recorded are not in our collection. It will be interesting to see whether these are at Pt. Ellice House when that collection is once again accessible. A by-product of my work in this and other photo collections was the identification of various of the "unknown" photographs at Pt. Ellice, thus adding to the documentation of that collection.

Also of value to this project were the magazines at the house, certain ones of which I borrowed. (The Appendix includes a list of the magazines.) These contained advertisements for clothing, as well as articles on styles, dressmakers and stores, accessories, activities, and people. They helped my understanding of the cultural setting in which Kathleen, and her clothing, existed, besides affording information on the clothing itself. I also found in them information about several different areas of Victorian life that was applicable to work outside this research, and I was able to get material for talks and school programming as a result.

Other documentary sources at Pt. Ellice were useful, in particular: accounts and bills describing clothing bought, and noting what stores were patronized; diary entries mentioning activities and people, and sometimes actual references to clothing, dressmakers and sewing; and notebooks listing clothing, store names, accessories, laundry, and mending. The invitations and calling cards again noted particular people and activities, both subjects of use to a study such as this, providing information on clothing. Choice of clothing is influenced by the occasion at which it is worn and by the type of people with whom the wearer associates. Knowing what Kathleen did, and with whom, gives us an idea of the type of clothing that we should expect her to wear. The bulk of material relevant to this question was in other repositories, notably the B.C. Archives and Records Service, with some also in the Victoria City Archives and Special Collections in the University of B.C. library. I consulted all of these, but found the most material and thus did the most work in the B.C. Archives and Records.

2.   B.C. Archives and Records Service (BCARS)

a. Manuscript Section (MSS)

Working with the O'Reilly papers in the BCARS was an undertaking of some complexity. Apart from the Vertical File (now in the form of horizontal films) consisting mostly of newspaper clippings on many topics and people in B.C. history, there are two main collections of O'Reilly Papers: the original collection acquired in the 1960s during Willard Ireland's time as Provincial Archivist, and the Additional Manuscripts obtained when Pt. Ellice House was purchased by the province in 1975. This latter collection consists of eight large boxes, each about five inches deep. Along with the earlier collection, it takes up about 30 linear feet of shelf space, and even this figure implies a smaller collection than is actually the case, for only two boxes hold Peter O'Reilly's diaries—over 40 years of writing and about 13,000 pages of entries.[5]

Needless to say, this is a mammoth collection to work on; however it is immensely valuable and productive to do so. The whole is to be re-catalogued at some time in the future, and better organized and integrated.[6] For now, using it takes time and work. Should one want, for example, a letter from Caroline O'Reilly describing her shopping, one must look first in the main collection, in her "Correspondence Out". But this correspondence is arranged by recipient, and as she wrote to her mother, her two brothers, her two sisters, her nieces, her two sons, her husband and her daughter, as well as to some friends, all these files must be checked. Then the same must be done in the Additional MSS. Each collection has "miscellaneous" files, which may contain fragments of such letters that were not put with the whole when first catalogued; these must also be searched. Depending on the date of Caroline's letter, her correspondent's answer may be in the Victoria City Archives, or in Vancouver at UBC.

Of course, almost all the letters and most of the other documents are handwritten and it takes a while to be able to decipher them. The Trutch family (Caroline was a Trutch) seems to have been very economical with stationery and postage. Their letters are regularly "crossed":

written—usually on onionskin—first on one side of a page in one direction, then turned at right angles and written on the same side again, and then the process repeated on the reverse of the same page. Accordingly, each page can have four lines of writing on it, on thin paper, frequently in poorly blotted ink, and in a hand that one must learn (Figure 1). The frustration that present day researchers experience in reading such documents at least may bring them closer to the past. Peter O'Reilly must have felt similarly frustrated for in 1888 he wrote to Caroline, "Don't cross your letters."[7]

There are also the "Correspondence In" files of those people who wrote to the O'Reillys. A particular document can be found in these if one knows whose name to look up, but otherwise there is no way into this collection, not even the possibility of knowing how many boxes there are of such papers, short of going to the shelves on which they are stored and counting them. I was allowed to do this, and thus learned how large the whole collection is. But we often do not know who wrote to the family, and the only way to find this out is to go through the Papers box by box; and because the collection is only catalogued by file within the boxes, one does not know what box to call for unless one is looking for a specific name known to have a file in that box—and how would they know that unless they knew who was wanted in the first place? Then too, the contents of these boxes are arranged alphabetically by author. Thus, a letter sent to Peter in 1860 may be filed next to a Great War letter written to his son. One must go through all the boxes, from names A to Z, to find all the correspondence relating to any one recipient.

Increasing familiarity with the handwriting made it possible to put together some separated parts of letters. More such work should result when the whole collection has been read. By the time it was necessary to stop the collecting of information, I had gone through about half of the BCARS collection, not counting Peter O'Reilly's diaries. To be sure, there were a number of items that had no bearing on my projects, and those were glanced at quickly and left. To put what I have achieved in some perspective, it should be noted that Michael Zarb, who was curator at Pt. Ellice for 10 years, estimated it would take at least six months' full-time work to read completely the O'Reilly papers at the provincial archives.[8]

It should not be necessary to say that one cannot short-cut the system by getting only those materials that deal with clothing, or cooking. The collection is simply not arranged that way, nor so referenced in the catalogue. Such is the nature of working with primary sources. It should be made clear that this, along with comments on the other collections I consulted, is not intended as criticism. Cataloguing cannot always foresee the needs of retrieval, and these papers are to be improved, as I have said. But the present system, here and elsewhere, does affect the accessibility of the information in the collections and the speed with which work on them can be done.

As with the Pt. Ellice House material, there was information to be found in a number of sources in the provincial archives. Some of the letters contain detailed descriptions of clothing styles, fashion, fabrics, dressmakers, stores, and shopping. Diaries and notebooks also had similar useful information, as well as listing sewing supplies and laundry. There is a much larger body of accounts and bills in the archives than in Pt. Ellice House, although even these are not complete for the whole of the family's life. From them I got names and addresses of dressmakers and stores, in B.C. and England, and descriptions of the items bought. In some cases they were very detailed, almost like a catalogue entry (Fig. 2), and were of much help in trying to locate that piece in our collection.

This collection also contains ball and concert programmes, calling cards, greeting cards, and business cards, thus documenting people and activities—the social context of the clothing. There were various miscellaneous items of help: poems, games, shipping and passenger lists, school and religious notes, spa tickets, and even some fabric swatches. Of particular interest were some sets of measurements for Kathleen and her mother, the latter dated and altered when Caroline had apparently put on weight.[9]

b. Visual Records Section

There was some visual material among the MSS collection, as well as in the Vertical File, which latter I was fortunate to consult while it was still a file. The films that have replaced it are in negative, so that it is difficult to guess from the films what a person looked like unless one knows beforehand. Of more use was the Visual Records section of the BCARS, where I found a number of photographs of the family and some group ones of which the O'Reillys were a part in other collections. In this part of the research again, there were obstacles. The present cataloguing is arranged by person, and so one must know a name in order to look up a file. But in group photographs, under one person's name, there may be O'Reillys not otherwise cross-referenced. Thus, some work on establishing the family's friends and associates was necessary in order to locate such photographs.

Then too, the photographs are not filed by the collections of which they are a part. I found in checking the photograph numbers with the B.C. Archives' accession records that certain photographs of the family had come from the O'Reilly collection, and that O'Reilly photographs were in others' collections. Possible sources of O'Reilly photos opened up in this way. Also, the original photographs often have information on them that does not appear on the copies in the files that the public may use. The photographer's name and address, as I have discussed above, may be extremely informative. Frequently, the copy in the file is of the image only and does not include the mount surrounding the photo on which this information is printed. Often that information is not entered in the photo file.

Furthermore, some photos have inscriptions on their back with names, places and dates. Frequently, this has not been added to the copy in the public file, but even if it has, the handwriting on the original has not been reproduced. It is important to know who wrote such information as well as what was written, for this is an important part of the history of the photograph. Knowing, for example, that the only portraits of Robert Falcon Scott (of the Antarctic) in the BCARS came from the O'Reilly family, and that the writing on the back is in Kathleen's hand, tells us of the relationship between the subject and the person who wrote. This supports other information on Kathleen's friendship with Scott, information that relates to activities in which she participated and to clothing that she wore. It must be remembered that when we talk of a person, for the most part we are talking of that person clothed and thus a number of different kinds of sources may be informative on clothing.

I was fortunate to have access to the originals in the Visual Records section, although time did not permit completing my research in them. I was, however, able to get some necessary information on photographs and inscriptions. Once more I found photographs that showed clothing in our collection although, again, there were many clothes that we do not have. Some of these may be at Pt. Ellice House. It may also be that, as many of those in the pictures are day dresses of wool or cotton, they did not last or were not saved. Those in our collection, being finer pieces and mostly of silk, were of a type that were not so often photographed.

I was fortunate in finding some photographs that until then were not available in the public files. Two notable ones showed Kathleen and her sister Mary, shortly before Mary's death at the age of seven (Figs. 3 & 4). They were extremely informative, and not only because there are so few pictures of Mary that exist. The fact that the two girls are dressed identically in the pictures says a great deal about how they were regarded and treated in their family. It was certainly common for sisters to dress alike at that time (Fig. 5), but until these photographs surfaced such information was not known about the O'Reilly daughters. It makes one consider, too, Kathleen's position in later years. There would have been two girls to play certain roles among the O'Reilly's family and friends; now there was only one. As the only daughter to be clothed and presented to the world, Kathleen had a wardrobe that may have received extra attention.

As was the case with the Pt. Ellice photos, those from the BCARS helped to identify clothing in the RBCM collection. For instance, a photograph of Kathleen as a little girl shows her in a dress with rosebuds on it, with a particular type of ruffled trim (Fig. 6). It resulted in bringing together two actual pieces, one in our collection (Fig. 7) and one at Pt. Ellice (Fig. 8), both of grey corded cotton, both with ruffled trim and with a small rosebud print. The one in the RBCM, although it has been on exhibit twice, has never had any provenance noted other than "source unknown". But this dress, so similar already to the Pt. Ellice one, although different in type of rosebud, was remarkably close to that in the photograph. More work needs to be done to establish when our example was made and for whom, but it seems most likely that it is an O'Reilly piece. Both dresses are handmade, and so they were not available commercially. Moreover, the similarity in fabric and trim makes it highly unlikely that they came from different families.

Another BCARS photo shows Kathleen holding a tennis racquet (Fig. 9) and wearing a dress whose eyelet hem is identical to that on a dress in our collection (Fig. 10). This latter dress was suspected to be of O'Reilly provenance as it has the same fabric—except of a different colour—as a dress known to be Kathleen's (Fig. 11). It is interesting that the known dress resembles in style one illustrated in a magazine ad to be used for tennis (Fig. 12). Similarly, other photographs have assisted in better identifying the O'Reilly pieces in our collection.

3.   Royal B.C. Museum (RBCM)

a. Collections

The RBCM collection also has its problems. It soon became apparent that finding the

O'Reilly pieces in the collection was not just a matter of looking up the donor-source cards that gave the O'Reilly accession numbers, and then proceeding to all their artifacts. The first problem here is that these cards name the donor, but the donor was not necessarily the owner of a piece. Thus, for example, to find Lady Crease's hat one has to know that Margaret Turner donated it. The many pieces that came to the RBCM from the BCARS have "Archives" given as the donor, and not the name of the original owner. Of those collections that are identified in the donor- source cards as O'Reilly, there are two main ones: 965.577 (210 listed artifacts) and 971.60 (184 listed artifacts). The former came in before the present Mrs O'Reilly went to Pt. Ellice, but its number is misleading. Usually, the first set of numbers in this system of cataloguing reveals the year in which an artifact was acquired. The 965 numbers in the History Division have in fact been given to anything that came to the Museum up to and including 1965, and also to some objects that may have come later but whose provenance is no longer known. Thus 965 has become something of a catch-all category of cataloguing.

The earlier 965 numbers, up to and after known collections like the O'Reillys', were applied to unidentified pieces, many of which had come to the museum from the BCARS when the History Division was set up and the Modern History Gallery was being built. Similarly, 965 numbers were used when the attempt was made to clear up the huge backlog of unaccessioned material in the late 1970s and 1980s; to this material, late (high) 965 numbers were given, from approximately .3000 on. This practice continues for those objects that have been here for ages and whose date of entry into the collection is not known. As my research progressed, I found that I had to know more about the 965 numbers than just the .577 collection of the O'Reillys', as it appeared that somehow this collection had spilled over into other 965 numbers.

The 971.60 collection is equally confusing. There are a number of pieces with Crease identification on them, which fact may show further evidence of the closeness of families in early Victoria. Just as they exchanged photographs, so too they may have swapped clothing. But stockings and nightcaps are not the same as photographs, and it would seem more likely that somehow two collections have become intermingled in this same accession number.

There are also some other O'Reilly pieces accessible through the donor-source cards: 965.1663, 965.1664, 965.3703, 965.3704, 965.3705, 965.3706, 965.3707, 965.4203, 965.4372 and 968.1, all with one artifact only; 967.168 with four artifacts; 968.6 with two artifacts; 968.7 with 12 artifacts; 969.40 with two artifacts; 969.72 with two artifacts; and 970.57 with 11 artifacts. Not all of these, it should be noted, are clothing pieces, but the great majority are.

There are even more identified O'Reilly pieces throughout the collection, but these are not readily accessible through the collections records as they are currently arranged. Some of the main catalogue cards mention O'Reilly provenance, but that information has not been entered on the donor-source cards. One would therefore have to leaf through the thousands of catalogue cards to find such pieces. Other artifacts have not yet been catalogued, but have labels on them identifying them as O'Reilly. In such instances, one would have to go through the collection piece by piece in order to find the O'Reilly ones. There were some pieces that I could not find in the collection although catalogued, and some which appear to have been catalogued more than once under different numbers.

Knowing the origin of these O'Reilly collections and their cataloguing history became of increasing importance as I realized that there were a number of pieces, usually with a 965 number, that were catalogued as source "unknown" or "not established (n.e.)" that were in fact most definitely O'Reilly. For example, there is the girl's dress that I have discussed. Also, there are two tea-gowns, both made by Howell & James of London, England having the same style, size and date: one has an O'Reilly number while the other is another "n.e." 965.11 (Figs. 13 & 14). I have also found "n.e." clothing very closely resembling that in photographs of Kathleen and her mother, and so their provenance should be reconsidered.

There are dresses having labels that I now know were from dressmakers for the O'Reilly women, as bills, correspondence, and other identified pieces have established. The likelihood of another Victoria woman of the same size and build, having the same taste in style, colour and texture and using the same dressmaker at the same time—especially when that dressmaker is in London or Boulogne-sur-Mer—is extremely small. From research in the magazines and discussion with other curators and collectors, I know that these particular dressmakers were not widely popular.[10] Thus, one may conclude that clothing with these labels belongs to the O'Reilly collection.

Going through the catalogue cards, I found more serious reason to identify the O'Reilly collections—and others—as clearly and perhaps as quickly as possible. Various items have been "removed/discarded/transferred" and even "destroyed". This has happened to pieces that, for reasons such as those just discussed, I can claim as O'Reilly. It has even happened within the existing O'Reilly collections (see example in Appendix). But until now, no methodical study of the O'Reilly pieces has been undertaken, and surely that should be done before parts of the collection are alienated from it, sometimes irretrievably. When the whole is known, then any extraneous pieces may be identified, if such exist, and dealt with. Discarding should not have happened yet, and should not continue.

One has to know the boundaries and content of a collection to analyze it properly. It turned out that as well as studying the O'Reilly clothing in the RBCM I spent a great deal of time trying to determine just what that clothing was. I suspect that there may be hundreds more pieces in the collection than are now so noted. As a result of this research, pieces were reclaimed from the "n.e." abyss and the possibility of being unwittingly de-accessioned, but there is much more to be done. This project concentrated on the dresses and bodices in the collection, which form but a small part of the total known pieces, let alone of all the potential O'Reilly artifacts. There is a continuing need to upgrade the documentation of our collections.

b. History of the O'Reilly Clothing in the Royal B.C. Museum Collection

To contribute to future work along this line, and to record what I learned while in the course of trying to establish the full contents of the O'Reilly collection, I will present the information I was able to gather on the history of this part of the RBCM History collection. These findings help in understanding how the present situation came to be.

The clothing was first bought by the O'Reilly family. Some of it came to the Province before Mary Windham O'Reilly's death[11], and more was obtained quite soon after she died in 1963.[12] Both of these acquisitions were apparently purchases, the latter being part of a larger one that included MSS, paintings and maps. The total cost of this was $10,500, of which both the clothing and the MSS respectively were purchased for $3,500.[13] The Archives correspondence states that there were 17 cartons of MSS and clothing obtained.[14] Inez Mitchell, who was Assistant Archivist at the time and unpacked the collection, recalls the containers as trunks[15], and the present Mrs O'Reilly says that they have a receipt for 40 boxes.[16] Whatever the number and nature of the containers, apparently there were as many boxes of clothing as of MSS.[17] This was a sizeable collection.

Although a letter from Provincial Archivist Willard Ireland to John O'Reilly in August 1965 says that an inventory of the clothing would be forthcoming on the return of Miss Mitchell[18], I was told by the latter that no inventory was done because there was not the staff, money, or time to do it.[19] Similarly, no cataloguing was done of this or any other clothing pieces that came into the Archives[20], other than by a piece of paper with the donor's name being pinned to the artifact.[21] Carolyn (Case) Smyly told me that at some point early in her work here as History Curator she was handed an envelope full of little pieces of paper.[22] These may be the same ones, at that time removed from their artifacts. Other families donated clothing around the same time as the O'Reilly acquisition, and Miss Mitchell recalled the Rithet, Pooley[23], and Crease pieces coming in.[24] Often only one item was donated at a time[25], but the Crease collection came in a trunk.[26] The latter fact may be of significance in explaining our 971.60 collection, which has items with Crease marking labels and which the catalogue cards describe as being found in the O'Reilly trunk; perhaps the Crease items got mixed up with the O'Reilly.

The clothing was apparently stored in the dome of the Legislative Buildings, above the B.C. Archives.[27] It should be remembered that although the Museum had existed since the 19th century, it did not have a history division. That was created with the new building in 1968, and then the history items in the Archives were transferred to the Museum.[28] According to Phil Ward, first Conservator at the Museum, the clothing was transferred even before the new buildings were finished.[29] They went to the building on Yates Street where he and the exhibits staff had their offices, a former car showroom.[30] The clothing, he said, was in very bad condition, very dirty, and full of insects. It was stored in an upstairs area on racks hastily made of scrap lumber, and treated liberally with "Raid" insecticide, all that could be afforded.[31]

When the Exhibits Building was finished (although the Curatorial Tower was not ready), the Government was eager to get all the Museum holdings out of scattered locations and moved them to the new building. The clothing was put into cartons and, in the absence of any other home, stored in a room in the basement near the truck entrance. Unfortunately, the new building had a good deal of trouble with water: the rain curtain, the main pipes, bad weather, and the sprinkler system, all at different times caused damage. There was apparently a flood a month for the first year or so. During one of these, the clothing was damaged by water and had to be treated. It was taken to a dry cleaner's in the city, and all that could be was cleaned and then returned to the Museum.[32]

The information explained a number of things. One was a story that I have heard ever since coming to the museum, from outsiders, that all the clothing (or only the O'Reilly collection) was damaged in a flood, and that some pieces were so mildewed that they were thrown away.[33] Most of the staff that I asked about this—and I asked many who had been here in the early years—knew nothing of such an occurrence.[34] Accordingly, I gave the stories little credence, other than noting how persistent such accounts can be. But one staff member did have vague memories of a flood that affected some clothing, and of subsequent dry-cleaning[35]; tracking this down led to the information from Phil Ward.

This history would also explain when the little pieces of paper were removed from the artifacts and, more importantly, why and how clothing pieces that were part of the O'Reilly collection became separated from the whole, and how other pieces may have become intermingled with it. If such were the case with this collection, what other ones may have become similarly jumbled? It would also explain why Miss Mitchell exclaimed particularly over how clean the clothes were when she saw them with me, and she repeated this when we talked on the telephone following her visit.[36]

When the BCARS clothing came to the Museum, it was not inventoried or catalogued.[37] Again, there was not the staff, money or time to do so.[38] Even when there was a history curator, Carolyn Case, the situation was the same. The priority was to prepare the Modern History Gallery, which was to be the first to open in the new building.[39] Further disruption to the O'Reilly collection may have come when this exhibit was being set up, as the selection of artifacts was often by trial and error: taking various artifacts to the gallery, seeing what might work, and then taking back to the storage all the objects that were not chosen.[40] Those that were not chosen were not catalogued but neither were many of those that were. Some had tags identifying them, and some of these tags I found in the History records[41] (Fig. 15). The cataloguing of the gallery was not completed until the 1980s.[42] The draper's shop in the Gallery is the one most likely to have received O'Reilly pieces, although there is clothing in other places throughout the exhibit. This shop was redone under Mary McMinn in the 1970s[43], and so its contents have not remained constant since their original installation.

c. History Collection Records

The BCARS material did come to us with some records, and these are among the files now in the care of Historical Collections. They are of some help, but are unfortunately very sketchy and need organization such as indexing. They consist of some donor lists and gift lists, as well as selections from annual reports. But there is a great deal more material in our collection than is recorded in these sources and, as items from the BCARS tend to be listed under that institution as "donor" in the donor-source cards, the name of the original owners of the artifacts, and of the true donors, have been lost. More work on these records, as well as further exploration of what exists in the Archives about our collection, may greatly remedy this situation. We are fortunate, in the light of this, that so much has been labelled as O'Reilly.

It is probably much of this BCARS material that bears the 965 accession numbers, both early and late. When, in the late 1970s and 1980s, the push was made to clear up the backlog of cataloguing, many pieces were done that had been in the collection for a long time. Such a situation was not unique to our museum, nor without reason here. The History Division was the baby, so to speak, of this institution and, at the very time it was being created, it had to create the first gallery immediately.[44] Understandably, many pieces came in that could not be treated with proper procedure—and that procedure itself was in the process of being set up.

We, like many other history museums in a period of centennial celebrations, were swamped with donations and most were taken, to be dealt with properly when more time permitted. And they *have* been, slowly, as time—and money and staff—has been found. In this manner, the exhibit artifacts were catalogued, and the backlog in storage has been reduced. In most cases, those doing the cataloguing were not trained or experienced in museology or history, but were summer students available through certain definite programmes. For example, there were a number of years in the 1980s when the students were here on an exchange in order to learn English.[45] They did so, as well as cataloguing for us, but the results were what may be expected of untrained staff.

Where we had someone interested or knowledgeable about clothing, the cataloguing reflected it in precise descriptions and recognition of the correct style, fabric and date of a piece. In some cases the cataloguer was assisted by some information either on the artifact—like a laundry label—or affixed to it, such as a tag bearing an earlier person's identification of the piece. In such instances, the backlog pieces have some information on provenance. For most of the pieces this is not the case; but one must not assume that these have no provenance, are therefore not important to the collection, and are the best candidates for de-accessioning. They may, in fact, be the worst candidates, for they came at the very beginning, have been here all this time, and many were here for a reason. The problem is that we do not at present know that reason.

But this does not mean that that reason will forever be unknown. In this project alone it has been possible to identify both early and late 965 numbers and thus rescue them from oblivion. More work on other parts of the collection should be equally successful; then we can decide what we should discard. It is the "babies on the doorstep", the pieces we are offered now with poor provenance or condition, or ones that duplicate what we already hold, that are the best candidates for de-accessioning. In fact, they afford the simplest way of controlling the size of our collection, and of managing it in the face of storage and staff limitations: don't take them in the first place.

Other records of the History Division were of use in trying to establish the scope of the O'Reilly collection. There are the "Old Catalogue" files of the years 1965-70. These contain some description of the artifacts that were assigned particular accession numbers. The handwriting of the people making the entries also reveals who did catalogue certain pieces. The "New Number" files for these different years also are of some help in locating items that came in the early years, were first catalogued under a different system, and later changed to the standard Canadian Museums Association one we still use. The labels of items that went to the gallery have been mentioned, as have the donor-source cards.

The catalogue cards were also of importance. Sometimes one of these would note that a piece was, or "probably was", O'Reilly, although not included in the known O'Reilly collections by accession number. During this research, I added annotations to the cards where I could establish a piece as an O'Reilly one, and thus their findings have been recorded. However, these cards are not yet readily accessible to those trying to retrieve such information.

(Over the course of this project, they were not physically accessible as a whole, having been taken to our warehouse to assist with work being done there.[46]) Looking for O'Reilly pieces, researchers will go to the most obvious file: the donor-source cards. To find items that are not within identified O'Reilly collections, they will just have to read through all the catalogue cards, although this should most likely be limited to the 965 set. There are at present about six thousand collections having a 965 number; each of these could have from one to some thousand artifacts in it. The catalogue is now in the process of being computerized and perhaps cross-referencing will be possible when that is completed.

I have noted that pieces of O'Reilly provenance have already been discarded both from the known collection, and from the "n.e." (donor not established) group of artifacts. In these cases, all we have is the catalogue card as a record of what is gone. Unfortunately, we might have had even more in such records than we have now. I was told by Mary McMinn that the typists who did her cards from her working catalogue sheets did not always copy all that she had written.[47] Thus, much more information was available on these sheets. I could not find her originals, and must conclude that they too have been discarded. It might help to have her come in on a short contract to see whether she remembers what she worked with while she was here, and perhaps to identify even more pieces as belonging to the O'Reilly—and other—collections.

The catalogue cards bear another source of information on the artifacts: their photographs. Where a piece has been transferred or otherwise removed from the collection, this is our only chance to know what it looked like. In studying the negative files of these photographs, however, I found them revealing in another way; it seems that there may have been some order and logic to how the pieces were photographed. I found a number of times that known O'Reilly pieces had been photographed sequentially close to ones that I suspected were also the family's, and to ones that I was able to establish through my research were indeed so. Mary McMinn had told me that she had originally stored the artifacts by collection[48], so that the O'Reilly pieces would have been adjacent to each other. The storage system has since been changed. It was disrupted during backlog cataloguing, as well as during attempts to make the best use of limited storage space, through storing items by size and shape. In this way the bodices, for example, are most likely to end up together, as are dresses, but the integrity of storage by owner has been lost.

If the clothing were stored completely by collection, it makes sense that the person photographing it would take it out in the order in which it was stored. I noted that not all the O'Reilly collection was photographed together—one does not find men's ties mixed in with children's clothing, nor women's. But there was a remarkable consistency within the categories of artifacts photographed, and more than once when studying a piece that for various reasons could be taken as probably O'Reilly, I found that piece among the identified O'Reilly ones in the catalogue negatives. Unfortunately, I was unable to locate the person who actually photographed this part of the collection but, though lacking that confirmation of my findings here, one can still make a strong case for the significance of the chronological order of photography.

Again, it must be said that in this description of the state of our collection and its records, no blame or complaint is being levelled at anyone. The reasons for such a situation are perfectly understandable, and I have tried to put them forth as they were told to me. We are not alone in having areas to work on in our documentation of the collection, as discussion of the other repositories has shown. A project such as this can be of help in pointing out the kinds of pitfalls that have emerged from past procedures, so that these may be rectified and avoided in the future. The study of the sources of information themselves was not at the outset a focus of this research but, as I hope I have made clear, it became apparent that it had to be dealt with if the actual subject of this study was to be attempted with any hope of success. As a result of my experience in this, we must conclude that a major consideration to be taken into account in acquiring collections is retrieval of the information that accompanies them, and the setting up of records that will make this retrieval possible years from now when the people with memories of the work have gone. Otherwise we have meaningless collections—and have neglected our mandate to record and preserve our history.

III   FINDINGS AND CONCLUSIONS

1.   The O'Reilly Clothing in the RBCM

a. Identification of Additional O'Reilly Items

With such a large collection a concentration of focus was necessary, considering the mass of documentation to go through and the limits of time. As has been mentioned, this work was concerned mainly with women's dresses and bodices. These pieces were the best to study, as they are the most visible in photographs, are unique in style, and identifiable by date. They are the most likely to have a store's or a dressmaker's label, and thereby allow one to learn more about the pieces by analyzing the businesses that produced them. Their measurements are most stable, for such items are not adjustable or made oversize as are drawers, chemises, and petticoats. The focus was further concentrated to a period from the 1880s to about World War I, although some information comes from earlier or later years to set this in perspective. In this way, I dealt with the period that is best represented by the sources, documentary and artifactual.

I have already written of some findings that had to do directly with the clothing. The identifying of various items as O'Reilly came in different ways and at different times, and almost always with some sense of satisfaction and excitement. A list of the various pieces that I was able to identify, with the probable owner of the piece and the information upon which I based my decision, is found in the Appendix. I will give some specific examples here, showing the different types of sources that made such decisions possible.

For instance, knowing that the Hares and Pinders were related to the O'Reillys, I did some research on these families. Among the documents, I found a newspaper notice of Carrie Pinder's wedding to Capt. Richard Hare in July 1874. Listed among the bridesmaids, dressed in "white muslin with pink and blue ribbons and sashes", were the "Misses O'Reilly".[49] At that date, Kathleen would have been about 7-1/2 years old, and her sister Mary, just over 5-1/2 years. We have in our collection two little girl's dresses, one smaller than the other, from the early 1870s, of gauze-like white fabric and both until now "n.e." They are of the right date and difference in size, the correct style for both the period and function, and one has mauve-pink sash and neck trim while the other has the same in electric blue—both typical fashionable shades of these colours for that time. Then too, their accession numbers are close to each other, and to known O'Reilly pieces. It seems a reasonable conclusion that these were the dresses referred to in the clipping, and that these pieces are O'Reilly (Figs. 16 & 17).

Earlier in this report I mentioned a photograph that helped in identifying the rosebud print dress in our collection; other photographs were similarly useful. In two that showed a group of people at a garden party or reception I was able to identify one of Kathleen's brothers and, after some study, decide which figure had to be Kathleen, given her build and age at the time. In one version of this photo, she was in profile, and in the second she was facing front but had moved. Her dress was eye-catching: a pale background with dark polka dots, the large sleeves of the mid-1890s, a deep lace collar, a large dark ornament on either side of the high neck with the same on either side of the front, and a wide dark waistband (Fig. 18). In our collection we have a pale blue corded cotton bodice, with black polka dots, and the same sleeves and lace trim, a wide black ribbon waistband, and rosettes of black ribbon in the same locations as the decorations in the photograph (Fig. 19). With a unique piece one can be sure that this is the one depicted and definitely O'Reilly; indeed, subsequent research located a copy of the same photograph in the BCARS with a key on the back identifying her! What is more helpful in this case is that the setting is shown, as well as other people. We thus learn a great deal about how one of our pieces was used, with what accessories, and in what setting.

Photographs were also helpful in locating pieces that further research may help to establish as O'Reilly. For instance, there is a photograph at Pt. Ellice of Kathleen wearing a striped blouse (Fig. 20) similar to one in our collection (Fig. 21). It has an early 965, non-O'Reilly, accession number, and is among a group of bodices and blouses that includes ones now identified as O'Reilly. Upon preliminary study it seemed that ours was the blouse in the photograph, but further examination of an enlargement showed that the stripes are closer together in our piece. Still, we now have definite proof of Kathleen's choosing this type of garment, and that may be added to the other evidence in favour of this being an O'Reilly artifact.

As I stated before, one of my observations in applying the photographs to the actual clothing pieces was that many of the items shown in the photographs are not in our collection. Similarly, many of our pieces do not appear in the photographs I have seen. In response to this, I have tried to obtain other photographs of the O'Reillys and have had some success, especially in finding them in group photographs in other people's collections. This is an avenue that could be pursued in the continuation of documenting our collection and identifying as many pieces as possible. Equally, knowing what is in the available photos, one can continue to watch for these particular pieces in our collection, and will know what to look for when the Pt. Ellice collection is once more accessible.

The magazines at Pt. Ellice House also contained visual material useful in studying the O'Reilly clothing. Most of these magazines were English, and one had a feature on the Drawing Room at Dublin Castle that included a photograph of Kathleen in her Presentation gown (Figs. 22 & 23). We have this gown in our collection, although comparison of it with the photograph shows that it has been altered from its original form (Fig. 24). The photo in the Archives shows the dress in profile, while that in the magazine shows it from the front; thus we gain further helpful information.

In some cases advertisements had been cut out of the magazines, leaving a hole in the original. Fortunately, issues of other magazines contained the same ad, and thus I could learn just what it was—and from what store—that had caught the reader's particular attention (Figs. 25 & 26). In one case (Fig. 27) I was lucky enough to find the original clipping itself in a letter, used to illustrate the type of dress that Caroline wanted her daughter to order for her in England (Figs. 28 & 29). That dress subsequently made by their regular dressmaker, Scotter, is in our collection (Fig. 30), and this information also helped my identifying the owner of the piece as Kathleen's mother.

Another advertisement showed a blouse with a very distinctive collar of petal-like pieces, and a smocked yoke and cuffs (Fig. 31). This is almost identical to a piece in our collection, again "n.e." (Fig. 32). Finding this ad is significant: first, for we are inclined to think today that any piece with such needlework was hand-made and therefore home-made; now we know that such work was manufactured, and commercially available. And second, it is of a colour, size, style and fabric to be considered as one of Kathleen's. The store that advertised the blouse is also one at which she shopped, and the piece was advertised in a magazine that had received sufficient attention to have had clippings cut from it. It is also interesting to note that the same ad shows a striped blouse like the ones discussed above (Figs. 20 & 21). A list of the items suspected to be O'Reilly ones, although not yet definitely so identified, is given in the Appendix.

The magazines helped to expand entries in the MSS sources that were frequently little more than a word or a line, and in so doing explained much. For example, a reference "Waterproofs-Cording's" became understandable when I found advertisements for a company of that name well known for its waterproofs (Fig. 33).[50] Similarly, in discussing where Kathleen should get her riding habit, her mother wrote of a business (whose name looked like Wolverhausen), that she said had been the best when she had gone to school in London.[51] I subsequently found ads for Wolmershausen, who made for ladies who rode in Rotten Row[52], and this confirmed what Caroline had meant; it also helped to establish the social status of the business to which she referred.

More detailed information than the occasional name or phrase was found in the Archival material. Many of the letters have lengthy descriptions of clothes being made and some, as I have mentioned, even contain fabric swatches. Thus far, none of those have matched any actual clothing that we have, but the descriptions have helped in identifying pieces or in adding information about those we already know as O'Reilly. The letters, notebooks and diaries frequently mention dressmakers and store by name, and thus one knows what labels to look for in actual pieces. The vast collection of accounts includes many bills for such businesses: of the various categories that the bills fall into, the largest number, after those for food, are for clothing. As I have stated, some of the descriptions on the bills are detailed enough to help identify clothing beyond just having a maker's name.

I was able to identify various pieces as O'Reilly by virtue of their dressmaker's label which, as I have argued above, can be considered distinctive enough to allow such conclusions. Thus a bodice of the 1860s, with Dulaquais label, could be identified as Caroline's (Fig. 34). This conclusion was verified by the fact that another piece with the same trim had a known O'Reilly number on it (Fig. 35). With store labels one could not be quite so certain, as obviously such businesses would have a much larger clientele. But other factors could help in clarifying the possibility of a piece being an O'Reilly one, such as size, colour, style and references in the MSS material.

In a few cases, people's memories were referred to in trying to establish O'Reilly pieces in our collection. John and Inez O'Reilly viewed the collection, and although our holdings pre-date Inez's involvement with the O'Reilly collection she had interesting supplementary information to offer, for example, that about the receipt from the Archives for the material that came from John. John himself did not recognize too many pieces, but it seemed significant that one which he thought was familiar was of a date that suggested he might have seen it actually worn by Kathleen, rather than just a cast-off stored in the house—and it was made by a dressmaker that we know Kathleen patronized.[53] Similarly, Inez Mitchell recognized certain pieces that she had dealt with when at the Archives.[54] That was almost thirty years ago, but she has not been looking at historic clothing much since, and so has not had conflicting information enter her memory. Also, she recalled a piece that I believed for various reasons was O'Reilly, even when a former Curator assigned it to the Wren collection.[55] But the Wren collection has a 970 accession number and came directly to us, not through the BCARS. Miss Mitchell had never heard of that donor and could not have been confusing the two collections.

Lastly, I used the study of the artifacts themselves, and in particular their construction, fabrics and measurements as sources in establishing the provenance of the pieces. I was assisted in the work on some of the pieces by Joanna Walton, who creates the reproduction clothing for the Parks Canada sites. She came here on a short internship in August 1988 and, during that time, analyzed some of the O'Reilly pieces in detail. With such study, I was able to reject certain pieces that superficially seemed to be O'Reilly but were unlikely to be so. In some cases, for instance, the measurements were too different from those of the known pieces. In this work I was also aided by the fortunate find, as I have mentioned, of measurements for Kathleen and her mother in the BCARS MSS collection. I measured our clothing at the same places in order to have some consistency and comparable data.

Much of this is not, in fact, comparable: weight can change, and in Kathleen's case this is recorded in her letters. Height can change too, whether one is growing up or growing old. Neck measurements vary with styles of neckline, back and chest measurements with the set of sleeve, and sleeve width and length with corresponding changes in fashion. Bust measurement and skirt or dress length seem to be more constant. The pieces that were radically different from the rest in these dimensions and that difference not explicable by the owner's age or a well-documented quirk of fashion such as especially short skirts at a certain time, were rejected as not O'Reilly.

As a result of my analysis of the clothing with reference to these different sources, I was able to clarify somewhat the boundaries of the O'Reilly collection and bring back within them certain pieces whose identity had been lost. I was also able to provide more information on pieces already known to be O'Reilly. An interesting and important result was that I was able to assign ownership of particular pieces more definitely; this had significant effects on my study of Kathleen's clothing.

b. Assigning Ownership to the Artifacts

Prior to my doing this work, the tradition had been that the bulk of the women's clothing in this collection—and probably much of the children's—belonged to Kathleen. Associated with this has been the traditional view of her as the much attended (implication: spoiled) daughter of an apparently wealthy family, to which the rich colours and fabrics of the clothes bore witness. I had had some doubts about this interpretation after working on the needlework and the information on the garden. The evidence from these areas was that Kathleen's palette would be a more subdued and softer one, not in keeping with the flamboyant colours and styles of some of the artifacts. Further research in the MSS sources seemed to support such a view. Kathleen was described as pretty but modest[56], and she herself referred to being shy.[57] Still, her clothes might have been at variance with such an image if they were what was fashionable, and the events to which they were worn required consideration of fashion above all.

But as a result of my research, it now appears that many of the pieces previously thought to be Kathleen's were in fact her mother's. Going by size and MSS references, it would seem that the dresses cluster into two groups: those with the more vivid colours, as well as rich fabrics and grand effect are Caroline's; the paler, pastel, neutral and natural colours—and less formal wear on the whole—are Kathleen's. My findings in this area are given in the Appendix, where ownership of the pieces is assigned to the two women. This discovery is more in harmony with the other information I have about both women, and it has various consequences. For one thing, it reduces the number of pieces that were regarded as Kathleen's and it makes necessary a similarly detailed study of Caroline's clothing. It calls for a reconsideration of the view of Kathleen's clothing being particularly opulent; such pieces were probably her mother's.

Then too, it alters our view of Caroline and to some extent of the older Victorian woman. In the photographs, the clothing worn by Caroline is dark and looks black. Indeed, what appears to be jet trim on various dresses would support the assumption that the dress itself was black. Further, knowing as we do how high the mortality rate was and the importance of mourning in Victorian days, we have come to expect that an older woman of this time would wear black.[58] Caroline, like many women, had reason to mourn: she lost her younger daughter and her mother within one day of each other.[59] Her letters show her to be an emotional and expressive person, but from the actual pieces that we have it would appear that this assumption of a long mourning period is wrong where she is concerned. One wonders how wrong it is for Victorian women in general, and how easy it is to stereotype the past. Caroline says (in the course of ordering new clothes) that she would order red instead of black.[60] So she obviously did wear black, and we do have black pieces in the collection, from her younger days as well. But her reason for changing colour is that she is tired of black and that red would wear just as well [61], and so there seems to have been no cultural reason for her wearing black. She also mentions how much she likes cornflower blue[62], and the most obvious conclusion is that she is talking of colours that suited her.

Upon reflection, it seems that her interest in such vivid colours might have had another origin. She was at the height of her youth when the new aniline dyes were invented that resulted in such bright colours as mauve, magenta, cobalt blue and electric green. It may be that a taste for such colours stayed with her. Kathleen, growing up when other colours were in vogue, had different preferences. There is also the fact that different sets of colours suit particular people's colouring. It had been confusing, prior to knowing who owned which piece, to imagine how someone who looked good in the off-whites and muted greens would similarly be attractive in the bright reds and purples. The fact of there being two persons' clothes represented here makes this understandable.

c. Alterations

In looking at the construction of the clothing, one naturally must study the alterations made to those pieces; these had been noted by others before. Carolyn Smyly's reaction on seeing them was that the collection was a mishmash of re-made pieces.[63] From Inez O'Reilly I heard that Mary O'Reilly, John's mother, altered the clothing for her own use, either as ordinary wear when times were lean or as fancy dress.[64] As Mary was of heavier build and shorter than her sister-in-law Kathleen, her alterations should be noticeable.[65] There was also the tradition that Inez O'Reilly herself altered historic clothing to wear as costume[66], but as our collection pre-dates her presence at Pt. Ellice that was not a factor needing attention here.

From my study of the clothing, as well as Joanna Walton's, we confirmed that many of the pieces had been altered, and many seem to have been hastily done. However, though a piece often looked crudely altered inside (Fig. 36), the overall effect, when the piece was worn, was perfectly acceptable (Figs. 37 & 38). There are a number of bodices without skirts in our collection and one must conclude that the great expanse of fabric in the skirts was used for other outfits. We have one example of a piece from about 1890 in the process of being altered to one c. 1911 (Fig. 39). There are a number of dresses that are in pieces, perhaps awaiting such recycling. At least one of these, it should be pointed out, was dismantled by a previous museum conservator, who left the Museum before re-assembling the dress (Figs. 40, 41 & 42).

The documentary evidence further records the procedure of altering clothing and very much explains it. There are frequent references to remaking clothing, either to bring it up to date or to hide damage resulting from wear. There is mention of "turning" dresses that are faded.[67] Alterations were also done on brand new pieces if the owner desired: Caroline wrote of taking out the sleeves of a new dress and replacing them with wider, more comfortable, and longer wearing ones.[68] She also asked for extra fabric, in a case where she expected that the fashion of a tight skirt would make hers wear out sooner.[69] Kathleen mentioned dresses left at her dressmaker's to be remade; her Presentation gown was such a dress, not a new one.[70] Its alteration at least once more after the Presentation is evident in the version of it that we now have in the collection. Bills also attest to the fact that dresses were regularly altered, and there are entries for "renovating" a dress[71] or making one from the client's own fabric.[72] Kathleen writes specifically of sending some cleaned pink silk for a skirt to be made up of it.[73]

The O'Reillys were certainly aware of spending money, whether through real need or just habit, at times when they were not noticeably in financial trouble. Caroline tells her husband in 1888 how she was unsuccessful in getting a discount either at her hotel, or at the chemist's.[74] Kathleen contrasts the great amount of money that the Dunsmuir daughters spent on their clothes, and the variety and amount that they bought, with the more modest wardrobe she would expect to buy.[75] It does not seem that the alterations were prompted merely by economic considerations; the practice seems to have been quite usual for the time. Most girls were taught to sew with some proficiency, and so all had some skill in working on their clothes.[76] We can find clothing in other collections at the RBCM that has been treated similarly. That of the O'Keefes' in the Interior of B.C. shows the same treatment[77], and literature of the period contains references to remaking clothing.[78] It is as if the original form in which it was bought was only the beginning of a dress's life, and it might go through many changes as long as it was wearable physically and acceptable in colour and texture fashionably.

The fact that we interpret alterations to clothing in a certain way may tell us more about ourselves. Women of our time are more likely to wear a piece of clothing unchanged for as long as it is acceptable, with not much alteration apart from the changing of hem length. But we are also less trained to do much else to our clothing and are farther away from the production of such pieces than our ancestors. Thus, change to clothing becomes a much more complex procedure for us.

At any rate, there was no particular evidence to support the contention that the alterations to the clothing mirrored financially bad times for the O'Reilly family or, as a corollary, that those were the only times when alterations were made. In fact, to support that contention we would have to have the clothing of the family's worst times—the 1920s and on. That is the very period that is not represented at all.

2.   Kathleen O'Reilly and Fashion

As reported above, I researched both the contents of our O'Reilly collection and the topic of my project "Responding to Fashion" in terms of alterations possibly being done as a result of financial difficulties. Such a perspective, however, looks at a relatively small part of Kathleen's overall response to fashion. In the course of the research I found material which informs us about this, material that helps to put the findings of this project into sharper focus and into its full social context.

What follows is not final, as there remains much to examine in the documents and, in particular, at the BCARS. Peter O'Reilly's diaries, which contain monthly accounts, are one important source, as are the mass of Caroline's letters to everyone other than Kathleen. The "Correspondence In" from non-family members has already produced valuable information and completing the work there would continue to be productive. For now, the following discussion can provide a foundation upon which future research can build.

a. Kathleen O'Reilly's Appearance

I looked first at Kathleen's appearance in order to understand better the clothing that she wore, and to have a clearer idea of the impact made by the clothing when it was worn. There was information on this scattered throughout the MSS sources, written both by her and by others. Interviews that I conducted helped in filling out this picture.

By the time Kathleen was 17 years old in 1885, she was tall and not very pleased with the fact. She reported that she was 5' 7-1/2", although she noted that this was when wearing her shoes (which would have had heels) and with her hair up on top of her head.[79] She said that she hoped she would stop growing, and called herself a "lumping big sister".[80] Evidently, a shorter build was the ideal for the time. Her weight seems to have fluctuated, as photographs indicate. At one time she calls herself "portly"[81]; at another, she relates that a doctor said that she needed to gain weight.[82] She said in reference to this that it was not a matter of her stays being laced too tightly,[83] and that is a significant remark about herself and fashion. There was much debate about the evils of tight-lacing as opposed to the stylish effect gained by it (Fig. 43).

Information on a person's health may also be revealing about her appearance. There is some discussion about Kathleen's teeth, and it seems that she had two—probably the eye teeth—that had never fully developed, for she refers to herself as "walrus".[84] More discussed was her skin: in 1884, exposure to scarlatina resulted in her face peeling, and she reported others as saying that she looked much better as a consequence.[85] A more long-term problem, although photographs do not reveal it, was a rash on her face for which various treatments were tried.[86] There is a possibility that this was eczema[87], although one doctor said that it was not. (He also said that it was not gout.[88] This latter seems to have been a common diagnosis in those days.[89])

Her skin was better in Scotland than London[90], and it may have been worse in B.C. There is discussion of her dreading to return here and become sick again,[91] and Caroline talks of giving her claret and water as a tonic.[92] There were also various illnesses in Victoria in those days, from reactions to heavy smoke[93] to diphtheria, fevers and colds.[94]

Her eyes were reported as grey-blue in her later years[95], although there may have been some change with aging. This may have been a family trait, for she refers to her brother Jack's eyes being such a bright blue.[96] Her hair was apparently a light or medium brown; her mother talks of Jack's and Mary Augusta's hair as "bright"[97] by which she seems to have meant "blonde", but this term is not applied to Kathleen's. Kathleen gave the impression of being tall[98] and slim[99], even despite some fluctuations in weight. We know that she had erect posture[100], a point that her father inquired about frequently.[101] To achieve this, she and the other girls at her school in England spent half an hour a day lying on a backboard.[102] She also moved gracefully[103], and again much of this was learned during her time at school through dancing, riding, and gymnastics lessons.[104]

Other people wrote about her gracefulness, prettiness and charm.[105] Various of the people that I interviewed talked of her sweetness, liveliness and sense of fun.[106] She appeared to be "well bred" although not snobbish[107], and she was described as being stylish[108] and elegant.[109] She herself was often disparaging about her looks, and there is some exchange between her and her parents repeating the line "pig, pig go away, I don't want you", probably an expression of rejection from a child's game.[110] She also talks of feeling shy in company[111], which reaction her mother praised, while encouraging her to act naturally and forget herself.[112] Her schooling in England probably reinforced her speaking with an English accent[113], and it was noted that this education was successful in "removing that nameless something which you and I know as 'colonial' ".[114]

Information on Kathleen's appearance also informs us about her clothing. Height and build are of obvious use in trying to identify which clothes were hers. Knowing her colouring helps us to understand her choice of colours in clothing; even though fashion may dictate a certain colour, one may have some choice of suitable hue. This information also helps us to be even more confident about which pieces belonged to her, and which to her mother. It is an added factor, too, in trying to identify O'Reilly pieces in the "n.e." artifacts.

Knowing how Kathleen moved and acted helps us to understand how these artifacts clothed her, and how they appeared when animated by such a person. It accordingly gives a more complete picture of them. In museum storage we see the pieces flat and stationary, yet clothing in reality is three-dimensional and mobile. In general, descriptions of a person's appearance are very much descriptions of their clothing, and can be taken to indicate awareness of fashion and success in choosing stylish garments.

b. Activities and People; Social Implications

With similar reasoning, I looked at the activities in which Kathleen took part and the people with whom she interacted, for it was with others and at certain events that certain clothes were worn. When Kathleen was alive, not only particular functions, but particular times of the day determined what outfit would be appropriate: there were morning dresses, day dresses, tea gowns, dinner and evening dresses. Then too, what one wore to go outside differed from what was worn indoors. A walking dress would be shorter and more subdued for public appearance; something for a carriage could be more showy; and a dress for house wear could have a train. That the O'Reilly family knew and followed such customs is evident from the bills that describe dresses made for different functions. Moreover, Kathleen refers to times when she might have been inappropriately dressed, such as when she arrived at a house to find her luggage delayed. She was able to borrow some clothing, however, and was not embarrassed because only the family was there for dinner that night.[115] Staying at the home of a very wealthy family, she noted their lack of pretentiousness concerning clothing and said that the women dressed for dinner in skirts and blouses, just as she did at Pt. Ellice House.[116]

Photographs of people in groups, and at events rather than in a studio, are very informative about what was actually worn and when. In contrast with magazine illustrations and advertisements, a photograph shows the real, rather than the ideal, fashion. In this way we can see the extent to which clothing actually worn matched what was published as the most recent style. Although a studio portrait does show the clothing and its accessories, a shot taken at an event tells of the activity at which the clothing was worn, and in what company. Seeing the photo of Kathleen in the blue dress with polka dots, for example, tells us that it was made for outdoor wear in the day time (Fig. 18).

Other sources also document activities and people, often with specific mention of clothing. A letter of Caroline's describes in detail the outfit that she wore to a wedding, along with the clothes of the other women.[117] At least two photographs exist of Kathleen at her friends' weddings as a guest or member of the wedding party (Fig. 44). Notebooks and diaries also directly record or suggest various kinds of activities, as well as the people involved in them. The names of other people are significant for more than the mention of individuals; they also document the members of a group, the circle within which the family socialized and which, like every social circle, had a certain status in the community.

The BCARS material includes programmes for dances and other events, invitations, calling cards, menus, greeting cards, gift books, guest lists, and so forth. These all furnish information on people and activities. Pt. Ellice House has similar materials, as well as catalogues for sports equipment, games and gardening. The activities that one finds represented by these took place in England as well as here and obviously travelling itself was yet another common activity. Many of the same activities, with many of the same people, would be experienced in both places. But there were also differences specific to each location; I will summarize the various ones from the different sources on the O'Reillys.[118]

Writing from England, Kathleen mentioned her school schedule and changes of clothes for certain activities, such as riding, gym and dancing, as well as for meals and evening entertainments. On a later trip there, she took bicycling lessons, and there was discussion of the proper outfit for that, right down to the underwear.[119] There were certain clothes worn for shopping. There were clothes that were taken on visits to others' houses, whether friend or relative, either for a weekend or for part of the holidays.

In London for two years of schooling and subsequent visits Kathleen went to see, and often stayed with, family friends. She went to concerts, at least once to a hospital for the poor, and to various exhibitions. At houses in the country, she went for walks and to Church; she visited historic houses, and the beach; she rode, played tennis, croquet, went driving, paid calls, and accompanied others at the payment of bills and grocery shopping. She visited people for lunch, tea and dinner; the last of these was often followed by games or music.

She studied singing and piano so that she could take part in musical activities, and also learned painting and needlework. These, too, would be done during visits to others' houses in the company of friends doing the same, or talking. Kathleen also did mending of her brother's and her own clothes, tending to save this for the times when she was on holiday.[120] She spent a lot of time in writing letters and also in keeping records of her expenses; both of these were in response to parental requests.

A certain amount of time in England was spent in shopping both for herself and for others. Kathleen writes of going to various stores and dressmakers. Bills in the MSS collections further record her doing so, and document her purchases as well. Much of this shopping was done with the awareness that such items could not be easily obtained when she was back in

B.C., and so there was the necessity of getting supplies for the future. Equally, shopping was done for others at home, both family and friends. This carrying out of "commissions" seems to have been a common activity, at least for those of British origin. Family members about to leave England were sent long lists of items to get for themselves and others, and these included furnishings, repairs and groceries. Even as late as 1912, when transportation across this country was so much improved, we still hear of people in B.C. doing much of their shopping this way.[121]

Many of Kathleen's activities described above were pursued in British Columbia, although they would be somewhat different in a new society. The community was much smaller, houses not as old nor as grand on the whole, and the number and the quality of entertainments available outside the home were similarly reduced. But we find the same mention of visiting, although Kathleen understandably went to stay at others' less frequently in Victoria. There was the same popularity of croquet and tennis, of riding and drives; when here, however, Kathleen drove herself more. There was school attendance during her early years here, visits to the dressmaker, shopping, and Church and related activities. There were Christmas and New Year celebrations as well as birthdays and weddings with their associated giving and receiving of presents. Kathleen does not seem to have painted or done as much needlework here as in England (perhaps because she had other claims on her time in B.C.) although both her parents advised her to bring supplies for these arts with her for the long winter nights on her return from England.[122]

A notable activity that would not exist in England was her participation in the running of the home. Prior to her going to England, the sources note her taking part in fruit picking[123] and jam making[124], as well as having some share in the care of poultry.[125] She was brought back from her schooling in England before her full time there was up, in order to help nurse her father and to assist her mother.[126] In the course of making plans for this return, Kathleen was advised by her mother to bring back from England dresses that she could use in housework in Victoria.[127] Servant problems were a constant theme in Caroline's letters[128], and the women of the house here would have to be prepared to do whatever work was necessary.[129]

As time went by following her return to B.C., Kathleen seems to have become increasingly involved with running the house and taking care of her parents. This is particularly evident from entries in her notebooks, which show growing responsibility for the many areas of household management: laundry lists, furnishings needed, plans for parties, and so on.[130] Kathleen's name appears on bills as the one in charge of buying various supplies for the house, especially certain groceries.[131] In 1904, by which time her mother had died, Kathleen was the one who invited a house guest and made plans for his accommodation and meals.[132]

All of these activities, of course, involved clothing, and some required very specific dress. By knowing what Kathleen did, we know what kind of wardrobe she had to have. As a result, we can better interpret the use of the pieces in our collection as fitting such activities, and know what other kinds of pieces to look for in the rest of the collection. For example, one wonders where her riding habit is now —quite a lot of information about it is in the MSS sources. Similarly, there should be a cycling outfit, tennis dresses, outdoor walking clothing, travelling clothes and house dresses.

We may never find such pieces, but even knowing that they did once exist helps in putting our collection into perspective. We see that today we have perhaps what was most valued, what lasted best over time, or was in the best condition to warrant saving. But we also know that we do not have all that should exist, or even a representative remnant of the whole.

As far as the people with whom Kathleen associated are concerned, it would seem that she moved in fairly high social circles, although probably not the very highest in terms of the "Old Country". To some extent, this was the result of certain accidents, coincidences, and luck. Neither of her parents' families seem to have been of the highest classes in the English social strata. At best, they were upper middle class. Peter's father seems to have been in the military[133] but was Roman Catholic, which would severely restrict social mobility at that time.[134] Caroline's family seems also to have been professional[135], but her position was helped by the fact that her brother, Joseph Trutch, became B.C.'s first Lieutenant-Governor. His appointment was fundamentally political, but it brought with it contact with those of highest social status in the Empire: royalty, nobility, and others with great power.

The Royal Navy was the other "top drawer" group in late 19th century Victoria, with many of the officers coming from high-placed families in England. The O'Reillys interacted regularly with this group and made contacts that furnished introductions in England. Those in the Government House "set" might not have the wealth and possessions that others such as the Dunsmuirs might have, but their position had an acceptance, a validation that those who were merely rich would have to try to obtain in other ways and over time. Usual methods of turning economic position into an acceptable social one were to marry one's daughters into better-valued families, or to send one's sons to school with the offspring of the same.[136]

To some extent, the O'Reillys followed this pattern of attempting to strengthen a somewhat tenuous social position by themselves sending their sons, and later their daughter, to school in England. It should be noted that it was not an unusual procedure in itself for the English settlers to send their children to what they thought was the best schooling[137], but the choice of schools did have social significance. Jack O'Reilly entertained thoughts of going to Eton or Winchester; Kathleen's school was run by a Lady Murray, with attendance at the parish church in the charge of a relative of the Marquis of Lorne.[138]

Thus, in England, Kathleen had entrée into relatively high society. Her parents had met Princess Louise and the Marquis of Lorne when the Lornes visited B.C., and had become well enough acquainted for the Princess to invite Peter to dinner, and the Marquis to write him a letter of introduction.[139] The family was friendly with Sir Michael Culme-Seymour, who had been Admiral of the Fleet in Esquimalt and elsewhere, and hunted with the Prince of Wales.[140] In the 1890s, Kathleen went to Ascot with her uncle, Sir Joseph Trutch; in 1906, she saw the race from the Royal Enclosure.[141]

But she also socialized with others, relatives and friends, of less splendid position. She had the potential—given her contacts and helped by her education, as well as her behaviour and personality—to climb by marriage to the upper class. Her parents' position was at least quite secure in the upper middle class, which did show a gain over their beginnings.

This fact, again, has implications for our collection. One's clothing is most of the outer face that one presents to the world and, as such, makes a strong social statement. Even those who profess to know or care nothing about fashion make that clear by their choice of clothes. Knowing the kind of people with whom Kathleen associated helps us understand the functions of the pieces that we have.

The social meaning of the clothes is also relevant in studying their alterations. For example, it is not functionally necessary to change the appearance of a ball gown for a subsequent dance—the dress is suited for dancing no matter what it looks like. However, wearing something that others have seen before, or that is no longer the most recent style, says to others (in a group where such things are important) that one's taste, awareness of fashion, and financial well-being are somehow inadequate. Thus, there is pressure to have clothes that appear different and up-to-date, and alterations make this possible.

Following fashion, of course, is not solely a social response. It has its aesthetic aspect, although the decision as to what looks attractive is not made without considering others' reactions. Then too, people get tired of sameness in clothes, as they do in food and furnishings, but one cannot say that people of higher position get tired faster than others and hence change their styles more often. It may be more important for those who do have such position and a lifestyle that involves a great deal of social activity, to have a lot of variety in their clothing. At any rate, and for various reasons, it is obvious that fashion is very closely linked to considerations of social status. In talking of Kathleen's response to fashion, we are considering her response to certain socially dictated standards.

c. Shopping
i. While visiting England

In what way would these standards be set and conveyed to others? One source of them would be the dressmakers and stores that designed and sold the clothing. A related source would be the magazines that carried advertisements for such businesses, as well as articles about what was in fashion and where to buy it. In analyzing the clothing stores that are mentioned in the O'Reillys' correspondence, diary and notebook entries, and on bills, one finds a great many that were English, patronized especially for dress purchases. Then as now, different stores had different qualities of stock, and certain stores were regarded as more fashionable. Indicators of a store's status would have been known by Kathleen at the time. Personal referrals, as well as the reputation of a store or dressmaker as having a fashionable clientele, would mark some businesses as more desirable.[142] The location of a store was also an indicator of its status, as certain shopping areas were favoured by certain kinds of people (Fig. 45).

As well as being spread by word of mouth, information on the right places to shop was recorded in guidebooks and other literature. It is worth noting that two of the businesses that catered to the O'Reilly women, Howell & James and Waterloo House, are mentioned in Gilbert & Sullivan's *Patience* as stereotypical stores for the normal upper class young Briton.[143] We also know that Kathleen saw *Patience* in 1882.[144] Most likely she had decided where to shop beforehand, but it is interesting to see how her shopping pattern followed that norm.

The appearance of a business in certain women's magazines would also be significant for then, just as today, different magazines had different audiences. *The Queen, Ladies'*

Pictorial, Ladies' Field and *The Gentlewoman* were among those in particular designed for the upper class reader[145], and all of these are to be found in the Pt. Ellice collection. Various issues, as has been noted already, have been clipped (Figs. 25 & 27) or have marginal notations next to mention of friends of the family. Kathleen herself appears in one of them (Fig. 22).

Time and again one finds stores in which the O'Reillys shopped dealt with in these magazines, in both advertisements and articles: Barker's, Redmayne's, Peter Robinson, Dickins & Jones, Marshall & Snelgrove, Swan & Edgar/Waterloo House, Cordings, Capper & Moon, etc. Even one of the hotels at which they stayed is advertised (Fig. 46), as well as certain brands of soap and other household items. The presence of such businesses in such a venue would mark them as appropriate to the social group with which the O'Reillys associated.

The magazine illustrations are of use in showing what was available at the time, and by comparing them with the O'Reilly clothes we can see how closely the family did follow fashion's dictates. The similarity to these illustrations of many of the pieces in our collection is noticeable (Figs. 47-49; 50,51; 52,53; 54,55). Even advertisements for stores for which we have no record so far of the family patronizing, depict outfits remarkably like the O'Reilly ones. In various cases, as I have noted before, information in the magazines explains what were only brief cryptic entries in the MSS sources.

Kathleen's dressmakers are not as well represented in the magazines, but this does not mean that they were not high-ranked. They were much smaller businesses, for one thing, and referral to them was more likely by word of mouth. Many of the labels of these places bear the royal coat of arms, showing that the dressmaker made clothes for people who would attend functions at Court. Also, the addresses of these firms were in the prestigious shopping areas (Fig. 45). As a further verification we can note that one of these, Mme Louise, also received mention in *Patience*.[146] We can conclude, therefore, that Kathleen was informed of the most current fashions, and shopped where they were available.

ii.   At home in British Columbia

Not surprisingly, B.C. stores are not mentioned in the English magazines. In the Pt. Ellice collection there are a few local magazines, with advertisements for stores at which the O'Reillys shopped; for example, David Spencer's[147] and Angus Campbell's.[148] Again, bills and other archival sources document which local businesses were patronized by the family. In analyzing the clothing stores that are mentioned in the O'Reilly MSS, one finds that a great many of these were English, especially in the case of dress purchases. Such shopping was mostly done during family visits to England, but some was also done long-distance, either by direct correspondence with the dressmaker[149] or by having a friend or relative do it as a commission[150].

To some extent, this reliance upon English stores was not odd. As immigrants, the family shopped in the place that it knew the best, felt most comfortable in, and valued the highest. (Similarly, the O'Keefe family, originally from Ontario, purchased clothing from Ottawa.[151]) The O'Reillys did not have a high opinion of local stores, and their correspondence records the lack of quality and variety in clothes here[152], as well as the high cost.[153] To be sure, one had to add the costs of transport and Customs to the price of clothing bought in England. However, it seems that frequently such items were brought back by the buyer or a friend, and there are instances of clothing waiting to be brought out here until someone was available to carry it with them.[154] Thus, these extra expenses could be avoided. Furthermore, considering advice such as sending a few buttons at a time enclosed in a letter[155] and wearing all one's new clothes before leaving for home[156], there is evidence that conscious efforts were made to reduce Customs fees!

In the light of the family's view of B.C. stores, it is perhaps more surprising to realize just how much they did buy here. Certainly, Victoria was not completely "this far end of the world", as Kathleen labelled it.[157] There were stores of many kinds here, and enough of any one kind to allow the purchaser choice of which to patronize. Even in Victoria's early days, Edgar Fawcett could note a good number of businesses here.[158] Stores here could order from San Francisco, eastern North America, and England itself. The O'Reillys seem to have recognized this state of affairs. For the most part, they chose to buy directly from England, even items that seem relatively insignificant or services that could more easily be provided locally. For example, Caroline asked Kathleen to get her some frilling in England[159], and declared that a good black satin button was not to be had in Victoria.[160] She also sent clothes to her English dressmaker for alterations[161], but the family did buy such things here such as trimmings[162], sewing[163] and mending supplies[164]. They also purchased certain accessories[165], and had many of their clothing alterations done here.

Shopping in Victoria was not just a matter of making do. Here, as in England, decisions were made in terms of fashion. The documentary sources show that a number of different women in the area did dressmaking for Kathleen and her mother over the years.[166] The turnover of their dressmakers may on the one hand reflect the mobility of a frontier society, where people started in one field and moved on and up to others. It may also reflect a search for the best on the customers' part. Kathleen had some dresses made by Miss Macmillan[167], who worked for David Spencer's dry goods store[168], and who made for other families of note.

What was fashionable here was not only seen to be so in this limited community: a cloak that Kathleen bought in Victoria and wore in England two years later, was taken to be the latest fashion there.[169] Thus, although living and shopping in B.C., Kathleen was up-to-date in her style. She herself was aware that her colonial home was not necessarily a fashion backwater. When her classmates and teachers were speculating as to the sensation that Alice Ward would cause upon her return to Victoria from school in England, Kathleen said, "I have had to stand up for B.C. and say that there are pretty and well-dressed girls out there besides Alice."[170]

d. Awareness of Fashion

There is strong evidence that Kathleen was actively aware of, and concerned with, what was fashionable; a list of clothing requirements in her handwriting mentions "pretty and fashionable" (Fig. 56) as important criteria. The phrase "what is worn", meaning what was in style at the time, appears frequently in her correspondence.[171] When asking her English cousin, Carry Hare, to shop for her in 1892, Kathleen wrote that Carry must choose the clothes as she herself did not see anything here or know what was being worn.[172] When in England herself in 1896, Kathleen explained to her parents that getting a new hat was necessary, although she apparently had one that was serviceable, because larger hats were in style and hers was too small.[173] She reported to her mother in one letter in 1896 that red and green were all the rage[174], and in a later one enclosed swatches for two new outfits that she had ordered: one red and the other green.[175]

Kathleen showed discernment in what she chose, and did not merely buy what was the latest style and the most costly, which fact shows sophistication in her taste. She pointed out how the Dunsmuir girls shopped lavishly, buying a wide variety of clothes of high price. In contrast, she stated that would not do for her[176]. To some extent, there may have been financial considerations involved in this; as I have noted, the family seems to have been very aware of its expenses. However, it also seems that Kathleen and her brothers were not denied getting what they wanted—as long as this was phrased in terms of some need, albeit very broadly defined.[177] Indeed, the O'Reilly parents themselves suggested purchases that their children should make [178], partly to compensate up for their being separated from each other for so long.[179] Kathleen dutifully kept her accounts and apologized for their inaccuracies and her extravagance.[180] (The guilt always seems to have been expressed after the purchases were made.[181]) One must note Kathleen's comments such as those about the Dunsmuirs' shopping habits, and her own appreciation of a very wealthy family for not being pretentious in the matter of clothing. These instances show that her spending was not unbridled.

We can see from such information that Kathleen did respond to fashion in her own way, and also that she was successful in the choices that she made. Her success is also evident from the comments of others about her appearance, as was discussed in more detail earlier in this report. In consideration of the question of Kathleen O'Reilly's response to fashion, we can conclude now that she did follow it and was up to date in the styles she chose. To what extent she may have led would have to be established by comparing her clothing with that of her contemporaries.

e. Kathleen O'Reilly Compared with her Contemporaries

Photographs of women in the English magazines—and here we are talking of actual styles worn, rather than the ideal presented in articles and illustrations—show hairstyles (Figs. 57 & 58) and clothing (Figs. 59, 60 & 61) similar to ones in Kathleen's photographs. Photographs of women Kathleen's age in Victoria also show similarity in clothing and hair styles. Even one quite striking hat style that appears in a photo of Kathleen can be found in a photo of the Crease daughters (Figs. 62 & 63).

Yet, in a situation where she was dressed identically to another, as at Nellie Ward's wedding, Kathleen's style seems to come through and her presence makes a bolder statement than that of the other bridesmaid (Fig.44). Close study of her clothing, from analysis of the pieces in the RBCM, revealed a greater complexity in construction and finishing details than in many of the dresses of her contemporaries. This finding is the more evident when Kathleen's clothes are compared to those of lesser social and economic station. One can see a greater awareness of fashion in her appearance even as a child than, for example, Laura Ingalls Wilder (Figs. 64 & 65) or, in her late years, L.M. Montgomery (Figs. 66 & 67). It is significant that one woman in her nineties today still remembers Kathleen O'Reilly's beautiful clothes and, as she puts it, if Kathleen made such a strong impression on a child of six she must have been something indeed.[182]

f. Conclusion

In conclusion, we can say that Kathleen O'Reilly had good clothes, clothes that were stylish from fashionable stores in England, as well as successfully competing B.C. shops. Her clothes were similar to those worn by others in her social group, and differed as theirs did from the clothing of those in other social groups. She was not in the financial position to have the most expensive clothing, nor of the personality or social status to wear *avant garde* styles. Yet she had a distinctiveness in her way of dressing that made her sense of fashion something remembered through the years, and her clothing among the many dresses in a large museum collection equally memorable.

IV   SUMMARY

In the course of this report, various areas and questions have been dealt with. Information has been presented about the different repositories and holdings that have to do with the O'Reillys, with note made of organizational circumstances in each one that may affect the progress of research such as this. In the RBCM in particular, one must consider the present state of the records on the collection and the needs that these may be called upon to meet. Similarly, the needs that the collection itself may be required to meet should be dealt with so that it is accessible for study, both by staff and by outside scholars. This situation is the more pressing when the results of such studies have direct consequence for the improved documentation of this very assemblage of artifacts.

As a result of my work on the artifacts, I was able to determine somewhat the contents and extent of our O'Reilly clothing collection. Within that collection, I was able to clarify the ownership of particular items, a finding which had important implications for our understanding of the individual artifacts and their respective owners. As a result of work in visual and MSS documentary sources, I was able to identify pieces that may be found in future, either in Modern History's holdings already, or outside them. As has been stated, in the course of this project I focussed upon women's dresses and bodices. Those in the RBCM collection that have to date been identified as O'Reilly are mainly of silk, and many are for evening or other more formal occasions. There are relatively few cotton or wool pieces, perhaps because they did not last as well, or were not considered as worthy of being saved.

I dealt with clothing largely from the 1860s to World War I. The collection at Pt. Ellice House has some more pieces from the 20th century, as well as a larger collection of accessories such as gloves, flowers, stockings, sleevelets, etc. I have pointed out that many of the photographs show clothing that has not been found in either collection. Also, many of the different activities in which we know Kathleen participated required clothes that are similarly not represented at the museum or the site: future work may produce these missing pieces.

The alterations to the dresses did not seem to be related to times of financial difficulty. Such changes, repairs and renovations were part of the normal life of the clothing, in Kathleen's family and in others. Taking fashion in its broader sense, I discussed the origins of the models of fashion and the extent to which Kathleen O'Reilly followed them.

There is still work that could be done on this topic, and suggestions for future directions to this research have been made in the course of this report. The main concerns are to complete the study of the archival sources, and to continue to identify and document the Royal B.C. Museum's clothing in order to realize the goal of knowing what exactly is in the O'Reilly collection. It is to be hoped that de-accessioning would be suspended until that goal is reached.

V   OUTLETS FOR THIS RESEARCH

During the progress of this project my research was called upon for various purposes additional to the topic under study. Many of these have been referred to in the course of this report. Here, I will draw them together, along with others that have not been mentioned thus far.

1.   In this Report

For the Royal British Columbia Museum:
1. Information for talks, including Speakers Tour, e.g., *Home Life at the Turn of the Century,* and a talk on Pt. Ellice House.
2. Information on school programs, *City Life, Country Life; Feasting.*
3. Information for docent training, which included a tour of Pt. Ellice House.
4. Material for Wild Plant Day, including participation of Cyril Hume, period landscape consultant, responsible for the garden restoration at Pt. Ellice House.
5. Two different Insight Booth programs.
6. Participation in Newcombe Auditorium program on Pt. Ellice House.
7. Identification and documentation of other parts of the RBCM collection.
8. Information for inquiries on Victorian history clothing, Pt. Ellice, and the O'Reillys.
9. Advice on high school research projects on the O'Reillys.
10. Interview about the O'Reillys, clothing, Christmas: *CBC, Times-Colonist,* Cable T.V.
11. Preparation, participation in programme on Kathleen O'Reilly for *Amazing Stories from the Fannin Foundation.* Also provide information to Art Gallery of Greater Victoria, Craigdarroch Castle and Victoria Rediscovery Society.

For the Heritage Conservation/Properties Branch:
1. Referral to Colleen Wilson, clothing and textile conservator, Royal B.C. Museum: to consult on treating the moths at Pt. Ellice House.

2. Advice on interpretation activities for Pt. Ellice House.
3. Advice on Christmas programmes, kitchen and food programs for Helmcken House (historic site, Victoria, B.C.).
4. Training of guides for Helmcken House, Pt. Ellice House.
5. Tours of Pt. Ellice House.
6. Provision of information from my research to assist with the documentation of the collection at Pt. Ellice House.
7. Identification of photographs in the Pt. Ellice collection.
8. Advice on orientation videotapes for the historic houses in Victoria managed by the Branch.
9. Provision of information found in the course of research relevant to archaeological digs at Pt. Ellice on the greenhouse and boathouse.
10. Provision of information relevant to the restoration of the garden at Pt. Ellice House. (Some of this was regarded as significantly changing the direction of restoration.)
11. Provision of information on the history of O'Reilly Collections.
12. Provision of information for Pt. Ellice House's participation in Fannin Days.

For the B.C. Archives and Records Service:
1. Information on MSS sources and photographs.
2. Information for Archives participation in Fannin Days, segment on Kathleen O'Reilly.

2.   Future Possibilities

Besides these outlets in which my research has been used to date, there are others that may utilize it in the future. Certain of these are not just projected applications of my findings, but have already been the subject of some discussion with the people concerned.

1. Training of the guides for the Heritage Properties Branch historic houses. This was made part of my 1990 work plan, and will be done three times a year.
2. Consultation on the re-cataloguing of the Pt. Ellice House clothing when it is unpacked. This was requested by Jennifer Iredale, Curator of the Heritage Properties Branch in January 1990.
3. Preparation of an exhibit of the Pt. Ellice House O'Reilly clothing, in the capacity of Guest Curator. No decision has yet been made on this request, proposed by Jennifer Iredale, in January 1990.
4. An exhibit of the Royal B.C. Museum collection, in our own space, which would get more return from the resources expended in the completion of this research project.
5. Restoration of Kathleen O'Reilly's gown, 965.677.43, completing the conservation left unfinished and restoring the piece to the whole condition that it was in when it

came to the Royal B.C. Museum. Colleen Wilson has already done a preliminary examination of the piece, and written a report on the work required.

6. Stabilization of Kathleen's Presentation Gown. This is very fragile, is an extremely important piece in the collection, and is frequently requested for viewing.

7. Upgrading of the cataloguing of the O'Reilly clothing, so that researchers can find all the relevant collections upon consulting the History Collections records. Data basing should help here.

8. Preparation of articles, talks and school programmes on the topics dealt with in the research: the O'Reilly family, Kathleen, clothing, shops and shopping, Victorian activities, the O'Reillys' social circle, the history of the O'Reilly clothing collection, and the procedures of this kind of research.

9. Preparation of articles on topics peripheral to the project, such as Christmas, children, servants, laundry, sports clothing, dry goods, etc. These could be the focus of several small publications.

10. Creation of sewing patterns, based upon the pieces in our collection that have been studied in detail, for programming or public sale. We are constantly asked if we produce such items. An O'Reilly pinafore has been replicated for the museum's exhibition on the history of education, June 1991; this would be a natural piece with which to begin.

Just as the richness and complexity of the O'Reillys' lives are reflected in the vastness of the sources that record them, so too are the possibilities of what may be done with these sources full and varied.

APPENDIX I
FAMILY TREE OF THE TRUTCH–O'REILLY FAMILIES

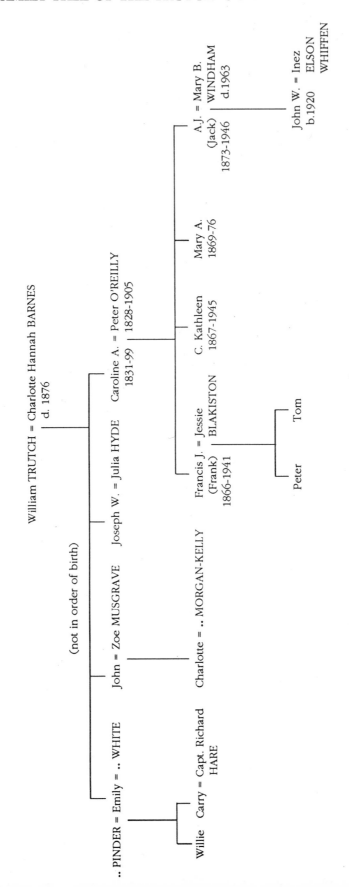

List of Magazines Borrowed from Pt. Ellice House

Modern Women, 1905, US.A. publication
Ladies' Home Journal, June 1908, US.A. publication

Miscellaneous Journals & Magazines, 1900-1920s
(title & grouping done by Pt. Ellice House staff)

The Deluxe Monthly Magazine, 1913, Victoria, BC
West Coast Yachting News, n.d., BC
M.A.P., 1909, England
Piccadilly, 1921, England
The Wide World Magazine, 1928, US.A.
The Famous Story Magazine, February 1928, US.A.
Sunday Pictorial, 1917, England
The Christian Science Sentinel, 1912, US.A.
The House Beautiful, 1913, US.A.

Miscellaneous Journals & Magazines, 1870s-90s

Bazar Fashions, April 1891, Toronto, ON
The Queen, n.d., New York
The Ladies Bazar, 1888, Toronto, ON
The World, 1891, England
The Court Journal, 1874, England
Public Opinion, 15 March 1879, England — one page only, 319-20
The Emigrant, 1887, England
Grip, 1890, Toronto, ON
Scientific American, 1890, US.A.
Army and Navy Gazette, England, 1890
Australasian Sketcher, 3 July 1880, Australia
Canadian Illustrated War News, 26 August 1882, Canada
Illustrated War News, 18 April 1885, Canada
Cottager & Artisan, 1874, England
The London Journal, c. 1856, England
Life, 31 December 1892, England
The Art Amateur, January 1881, England
The Illustrated Sporting and Dramatic News, 10 December 1881, England

Country Life, England

28 January 1899	5 April 1913	8 March 1946	16 January 1948
24 October 1908	12 June 1920	22 March 1946	26 March 1948
30 January 1909	27 August 1938	24 January 1947	9 April 1948
2 March 1912	6 May 1939	10 October 1947	14 May 1948
5 October 1912	17 February 1940	14 November 1947	21 May 1948

Country Life, England, cont.

28 May 1948	4 March 1949	10 June 1949
1 June 1948	6 May 1949	17 June 1949
18 June 1948	13 May 1949	25 November 1949
25 June 1948	27 May 1949	2 December 1949
25 February 1949	3 June 1949	

Figaro Illustre´, France/England
1891
1893
n.d.

Black & White, England
Christmas, 1891
Christmas, 1894
one page only of 16 January 1909, 73-4

Pears Christmas Annual, England
1894
1895
1897

Yuletide, Cassell's Christmas Annual, England
1891
1892

Miscellaneous Christmas

(title & grouping done by Pt. Ellice House staff)

Pearson's Christmas, 1895, England
The Graphic, 1907, England
The King, 1901, England

Holly Leaves, England
1891
1907
1912
1925

The Ladies' Field, England
12 August 1899
Santa Claus Supplement — the cover has 24 November 1905;
the inside has 24 November 1906
24 November 1906 supplement to the *Ladies' Field*
23 November 1912

The Gentlewoman, England
31 January 1891
Christmas, 1909
15 June 1912

The Lady's Pictorial, England
30 May 1890
21 February 1891
Christmas, 1891
27 February 1897
29 May 1909
26 October 1912
14 December 1912
1 February 1913

The Queen, England, 1890s (grouping done by Pt. Ellice staff)
14 September 1889
18 January 1890
25 January 1890 — only pp. 171-124
17 May 1890
7 June 1890
13 December 1890
27 June 1891
4 July 1891
Christmas, 1898

The Queen, England, 1900-teens (grouping done by Pt. Ellice staff)
24 November 1906
19 December 1908
27 November 1909
Christmas, 1910
Christmas, 1911
Christmas, 1912

Province of British Columbia

British Columbia
Provincial Museum
Parliament Buildings
Victoria
British Columbia
V8V 1X4

COLLECTION TRANSFER
Modern History Division—Form 10
Phone: (604) 387-3648

To: Mr. Ken Zurosky

Date: 21 November 1984

Fort Steele Provincial Historic Park

Fort Steele, B.C.   VOB 1NO

NOTICE OF TRANSFER

The following items are surplus to the Provincial Museum's modern history collection. Each has been deaccessioned and is herewith transferred to the collection of: Fort Steele Provincial Historic Park

ITEM	B.C.P.M. ACCESSION No.	
Woman's Drawers	965.577.13	O'Reilly
"	965.577.16	Collection
Woman's petticoat	965.577.18	
"	965.577.157	
Woman's drawers	965.577.170	
"	965.577.175	
Woman's bodice	965.719	965 numbers
Baby's dress	965.1176	may be
Woman's petticoat	965.1246	O'Reilly
Woman's black petticoat	965.1451	
Woman's drawers	965.1615	
"	965.1616	
"	965.1617	
Woman's blouse	965.1618	
✗ Child's dress	967.147.75	R.P. Brown
✗ Baby's petticoat	967.147.96	" "
Woman's nightgown	967.165.78	
Woman's petticoat	967.154.5	ML
Baby's dress	970.60.24	addison
"	970.69.4	
Woman's petticoat	970.103.5	Mather
Baby's dress	972.17.3	
Woman's skirt	972.134.2 ?	
Woman's dress	972.337.4	

Recommended: _____
Curator of Modern History

Approved: _____
Director

I hereby acknowledge receipt of the above items and am adding them to the Fort Steele collection.

✗ 985.01.09
cc   (Date)

_____
(Signature)

TABLE 1

ADDITIONAL RBCM DRESSES & BODICES
IDENTIFIED AS O'REILLY

Abbreviations:
K = Kathleen
C = Caroline
T = Mrs. H. Trutch
M = Mary A.

Catalogue #	Item	Probable Owner	Evidence
965.578	White eyelet tennis gown, c. 1880s.	K	BCARS photograph 50119; same fabric as 965.577.35, which is an identified piece of Kathleen's.
954.624	Blue Howell & James tea gown, c. 1880s.	K	Same make, style, size and date as 965.577.22, which is identified as Kathleen's and is in a known O'Reilly collection.
965.717	Black net bodice over bright green taffeta.	K	Bill is in Victoria City Archives c. 1898 Pearse Collection.
965.721	Pink faille bodice with black net, c. 1898.	C	Scotter label; bill for same in BCARS, O'Reilly Papers.
965.733	Green bodice/vest in midst of alteration, c. 1890s.	K	"Miss O'Reilly" in pencil on inside of collar.
965.734	Black bodice with purple floral print, c. 1870s.	T	Label of a known O'Reilly dressmaker, Braff-Dulaquais; size, date, style seem too big for Caroline, and Kathleen was a child at this time. Cf. article on Mrs. Trutch in N. de Bertrand Lugrin *Pioneer Women of Vancouver Island*, re: Mrs. Trutch's clothing preferences, p. 275.
965.766	Striped bodice with electric blue & black trim, c.1860.	C	Bears the label of a known O'Reilly dressmaker, Dulaquais. Size, style and date would suit Caroline (Kathleen was then a child). The same trim is on skirt piece, 971.60.94, part of a known O'Reilly collection.

cont'd

Table 1 cont'd

Catalogue #	Item	Probable Owner	Evidence
965.1422	Child's dress with rosebud print, c. 1870s.	K or M	Fabric and trim are not commonly found, and match closely that in a dress worn by Kathleen, (BCARS photograph HP50070) a similar dress is in the Pt. Ellice House collection, 975.1.2159
965.1423	Petticoat to go with bridesmaid dress 965.1437 c. 1870s.	K	Victoria *Colonist* description of Hare-Pinder wedding with the Misses O'Reilly among the bridesmaids; the ribbon on this piece is the same as that on 965.1437.
965.1434	White fancy child's dress with blue neck ribbon and sash, c. 1870s	M	Victoria *Colonist* description of the Hare-Pinder wedding, July 17, 1874, at which the Misses O'Reilly were among the bridesmaids, dressed in white muslin dresses with blue and pink ribbons and sashes. The size, style and date of the dress, along with the difference in size from 965.1437, are in keeping with Mary A's and Kathleen's relative ages.
965.1437	White fancy child's dress with pink neck ribbon and sash.	K	Same as preceeding.
965.4407	Black bodice, c. 1860s.	C	Bears the label of a known O'Reilly dressmaker, Dulaquais, and is the appropriate size and date for Caroline.

TABLE 2

RBCM ITEMS SUSPECTED TO BE O'REILLY*

Abbreviations:

K = Kathleen   F = Frank
C = Caroline   J = Jack
M = Mary A.

Catalogue #	Item	Probable Owner	Evidence
965.623	Dress with print of ivy leaves, wine sash.	C	Early 965 number; similar in style to 965.577.542, an identified O'Reilly dress.
965.635	White Indian muslin dress, black & white tambour work.	C	Inez Mitchell remembers it from the BCARS. Caroline was in India during the 1860's.
965.647	Blue dress, Lavigne label	K	John O'Reilly thought he recognized it, Lavigne was an O'Reilly dressmaker (bill in BCARS O'Reilly collection).
965.722	Plaid gauze bodice.	C	Inez O'Reilly noted its similarity to a known O'Reilly dress at Pt. Ellice house.
965.723	Pink bodice; Redmayne's.	K	From a store where Kathleen shopped; size, colour, style and date appropriate to her. Lining similar to one in an identified O'Reilly piece.
965.728	Turquoise satin blouse, black velvet trim, Peter Robinson.	K	From a store where Kathleen shopped; style, size, colour and date appropriate to her. Colour combination similar to known O'Reilly pieces.
965.730	Red & white striped blouse.	K	Very similar to one worn by Kathleen in a photo at Pt. Ellice House. Alterations similar to known O'Reilly pieces.

*This presents pieces for which I had some definite evidence. Many others might be included, with O'Reilly provenance suspected because of proximity in cataloguing and photography to known O'Reilly artifacts. This information also is limited by my studying primarily dresses and bodices. Although other types of clothing are mentioned in this table, I did not cover the complete range of the O'Reilly clothing on this project, and would expect a great many more suspected pieces were I to do so.

cont'd

Table 2 cont'd

Catalogue #	Item	Probable Owner	Evidence
965.762	Azure silk blouse with smocking.	K	Identical to one in an ad in a magazine at Pt. Ellice House; appropriate style, size, colour and date for Kathleen. We have evidence of her wearing a blouse like another one shown in the same ad. (see 965.730 above.)
965.882	Wine velvet princess dress.	C	Inez Mitchell recognized it from the BCARS. Has been altered like known O'Reilly pieces size, date, colour and style appropriate to Caroline.
965.1432 965.1441 (larger one)	Two children's pongee silk coats.	K & M or F or J	Early 965 number; proximity in cataloguing and photography to bridesmaids' dresses (965.1423, 965.1437); style, size, date and relative difference in size, appropriate to the O'Reilly children. Similar fabrics and style.
965.1443	Child's dress, coral ribbon trim.	an O'Reilly child	Ribbon similar to that on a known O'Reilly dress at Pt. Ellice House.
965.1447	Grey-yellow shot taffeta; R. Dale & Co.	K	Label from a store Kathleen shopped at; appropriate size, colour, date and style.
965.1665	Purple grosgrain and velvet dress.	C	Catalogue card information.
965.1963	Cape, pinstriped silk Bon Marché.	K/C	From a store the O'Reilly's shopped at; appropriate size, colour, date and style.
965.2161	Hat; Mme Wans.	K/C	Same label on identified O'Reilly hats.
965.2199	Hat, Mme Wans.	K/C	Same as 965.2161.
965.4293	Skirt(?) - blue-grey with black stem and leaf design.	K	Similar to one worn by Kathleen in a photograph at Pt. Ellice House.

cont'd

Table 2 cont'd

Catalogue #	Item	Probable Owner	Evidence
965.4298	Black brocade mantle; Peter Robinson	K/C	From a store Kathleen shopped at; Inez Mitchell remembered it.
965.4393	Green velvet mantle; Peter Robinson.	K/C	From a store the O'Reilly's shopped at; appropriate style and date.
965.4408	Blue-green bodice with dried grasses	K	Style, size, date, colour and trim appropriate
965.4898	Hat, c. 1900-10; Dickins & Jones	K	From a store Kathleen shopped at; appropriate style, date and colour.
965.4979	Bustle.	K	"Attributed to O'Reillys" on catalogue card.
965.5359	Parasol with parakeet handle.	K	Identical to O'Reilly piece in collection.
970.48.13	Brown print cotton dress.	C	A scrap of the same fabric is with other scraps "found in the O'Reilly trunk." This is assigned to the Wren Collection, on which the provenance is vague. Another supposed Wren piece 965.635, although not of the Wren accession number, was recognized by Inez Mitchell as coming from the Archives–and she had never heard of the Wrens.

TABLE 3

OWNERSHIP WITHIN THE ROYAL B.C. MUSEUM O'REILLY COLLECTION: DRESSES AND BODICES

Catalogue #	Item	Probable Owner	Evidence
965.577.22	Green velvet tea gown; Howell & James.	K	Size; date; identifying tag.
965.577.23	Black broché dress; Scotter.	C	Size; correspondence.
965.577.25	Black net over red, Scotter.	C	Size.
965.577.26	Black and white striped dress; Lavigne.	K	Possible photographic evidence; Kathleen shopped at Lavigne's; date of alteration post-dates Caroline.
965.577.27	Red velvet dress; Scotter.	C	Size; correspondence.
965.577.28	White silk dress with silver embroidery.	K	Date post-dates Caroline; size.
965.577.29	Brown-black brocade.	C(?) K(?)	Opulence; colour. Size.
965.577.30	Gold moiré, 2 bodices.	C	Size.
965.577.31	Red-black shot silk; Scotter.	C	Size; correspondence.
965.577.32	Purple velvet and satin with lace; Townsend.	C	Size.
965.577.33	Gold striped brocade, white fichu.	K	Size; may be one mentioned in BCARS bills, correspondence.
965.577.34	Pongee silk embroidered bodice.	K	Size, colour.
965.577.35	Cream eyelet, blue lining.	K	Size.

cont'd

Table 3 cont'd

Catalogue #	Item	Probable Owner	Evidence
965.577.36	Pongee silk, blouson top.	K	Size; date; post-dates Caroline.
965.577.43	Coral and black chiffon.	K	Size; date; photograph of her wearing it.
965.577.44	Black velvet bolero.	C	Photograph of her wearing it.
965.577.142	Pink silk with tiny print; red sash.	K	Style; size; date; correspondence.
965.577.182	Presentation Gown; Scotter.	K	Photograph of Kathleen wearing it.
965.577.183	Cream corded silk with pink ribbon; Scotter.	K	Size; style; archival documentation.
no number	White taffeta with run floral print, apple green trim, crystal beads - dress in pieces found in O'Reilly trunk.	C	Date; style; predates Kathleen.

REFERENCES

Abbreviations:

BCARS: British Columbia Archives and Records Service
RBCM: Royal British Columbia Museum
UBC: University of British Columbia
VCA: Victoria City Archives

1. Michael Zarb, former Curator, Pt. Ellice House.   Personal communication, Summer 1976; 10 March 1988. Inez O'Reilly (Mrs. John O'Reilly). Personal Communication, Summer 1976.
A.J. O'Reilly to C.K. O'Reilly, 11 August 1911; 4 February 1914. O'Reilly Papers, BCARS.
2. Colleen Wilson, Clothing & Textile Conservator, RBCM. *Report on Operation Moth & Other Concerns at Pt. Ellice House,* June 1988.
Colleen Wilson, RBCM.   "Moths, moths and more moths", *Museum Round-up,* #152. B.C. Museums Association, February 1990.
3. Inez O'Reilly. Personal communication, Summer 1976; 19 February 1990, 8 March 1990, 4 April 1990.
4. Michael Zarb.   File for Pt. Ellice House Guides, c. 1970s, at Pt. Ellice House.
5. Cyril D. Hume, period landscape consultant. Personal communication, Fall 1989.
6. Susan Hart, Archivist, BCARS. Personal communication, Fall 1989.
7. Peter O'Reilly to Caroline O'Reilly, 4 December 1888. Pearse Collection, Victoria City Archives.
8. Michael Zarb. Personal communication, Fall 1989.
9. C.A. & C.K. O'Reilly's measurements. O'Reilly Papers, BCARS.
10. Costume Society, London, England. Personal communication, 4 April, 1989.
Guildhall Library, London, England. Personal communication, 5 April 1989.
Mary Tunnell, member of Costume Society, London, England. Personal communication, 9 September 1989.
Mary Witt, member of Costume Society, London, England. Personal communication, 7 October 1989.
Ivan Sayers, Curator of History, Vancouver Museum. Personal communication, March 1990.
11. Inez Mitchell, Retired Assistant Archivist, BCARS. Personal communication, 1 December 1989; 28 March 1990.
Cf. Willard Ireland, Provincial Archivist, to John W. O'Reilly, 3 January 1964. Archives Correspondence, BCARS.
12. Inez Mitchell, 1 December 1989; Victoria *Times* obituary, 17 December 1963.
13. Willard Ireland to John O'Reilly, 23 February 1966. Archives Correspondence, BCARS.
John O'Reilly to Willard Ireland, 3 March 1966. Archives Correspondence, BCARS.
14. Willard Ireland to John O'Reilly, 3 January 1964; on 25 October 1965 note was made of five cartons being returned. Archives correspondence, BCARS.
15. Inez Mitchell. Personal communication, 1 December 1989.
16. Inez O'Reilly. Personal communication, 1 December 1989, 8 December 1989; 15 February 1990, 8 March 1990, 4 April 1990.
17. Inez Mitchell. Personal communication, 29 March 1990.
18. Willard Ireland to John O'Reilly, 27 August 1965. Archives Correspondence, BCARS.
19. Inez Mitchell. Personal communication, 28 March 1990.
20. Ibid.
21. Ibid.
22. Carolyn (Case) Smyly, former Curator of History, RBCM. Personal communication, 1 November 1988; 18 December 1989.
23. Inez Mitchell, 28 March 1990.
24. Ibid. 1 December 1989.
25. Ibid. 28 March 1990.
26. Ibid. 1 December 1989.

27.   Ibid. 28 March 1990.

28.   Dan Gallacher "Exhibits as Overviews: the Case of British Columbia Modern History" in Dave Richeson, ed., *Western Canadian History: Museum Interpretations.*   Mercury Series #27, History Division, National Museum of Man, Ottawa 1979. p. 11.
      Peter Corley-Smith *The Ring of Time: The Story of the B.C. Provincial Museum.*   BCPM, Victoria, B.C., 1985. p. 9. Phil Ward, former Conservator, RBCM.   Personal communication, 28 March 1990.

29.   Phil Ward, 28 March 1990.
      Carolyn Smyly, 18 December 1989.

30.   Ibid.

31.   Phil Ward, 28 March 1990.

32.   Ibid.   Whole paragraph.

33.   Canadiana Costume Society.   Various members, 1979 on.

34.   Dan Gallacher, former History Curator, RBCM; Jim Wardrop, former Assistant History Curator; Mary McMinn, former Clothing Curator; Carolyn Smyly, former History Curator, 1989-1990.

35.   Tom Palfrey, former Exhibits Division employee, RBCM, February 1990.

36.   Inez Mitchell, 28/29 March 1990.

37.   Carolyn Smyly, 1 November 1988; 18 December 1989.

38.   Ibid.

39.   Ibid.   18 December 1989.

40.   Ibid.

41.   Ibid.

42.   Virginia A.S. Careless.   Personal experience, 1980s.

43.   Mary McMinn, former Clothing Curator, RBCM, 15 December 1989.

44.   Dan Gallacher, Jim Wardrop, Zane Lewis, and others.   Personal communications, various times 1979-on.

45.   Virginia A.S. Careless.   Personal experience. 1980s.

46.   Bob Turner, Chief, Historical Collections, RBCM.   Memo, 13 September 1986.

47.   Mary McMinn.   Personal communication, 8 March 1990.

48.   Ibid. 15 December 1989.

49.   Victoria *Colonist,* 17 July 1874.

50.   C.K. O'Reilly, Notebook 1902.   O'Reilly Papers, BCARS.

51.   C.A. O'Reilly to C.K. O'Reilly, 18 July 1885.   O'Reilly Papers, BCARS.

52.   *Lady's Pictorial,* 3 May 1890.   Pt. Ellice House magazine.

53.   John O'Reilly.   Personal communication, 8 December 1990.

54.   Inez Mitchell.   Personal communication, 28 March 1990.

55.   Ibid.

56.   Agnes Murray to C.A. O'Reilly, 27 April 1885.   O'Reilly Papers, BCARS.

57.   C.K. O'Reilly to C.A. O'Reilly, 26 June 1885.

58.   Lou Taylor *Mourning Dress: A Costume and Social History.*   London: George Allen & Unwin, 1983.   See Chapter 6 "1800-1910" pp. 120-163.

59.   O'Reilly gravestone, Ross Bay cemetery, Victoria, B.C.
      N. de Bertrand Lugrin and John Hosie *The Pioneer Women of Vancouver Island 1843-1866.* Victoria, B.C.: The Women's Canadian Club, 1928.   p. 303.

60.   C.A. O'Reilly to C.K. O'Reilly, 12 March 1897.   O'Reilly Papers, BCARS.

61.   C.A. O'Reilly to C.K. O'Reilly, 23 March 1897.   O'Reilly Papers, BCARS.

62.   Ibid.   25 May 1897.

63.   Carolyn Smyly.   Personal communication, 1 November 1988; 18 December 1989.

64. Inez O'Reilly. Personal communication, Summer 1976; also Mary McMinn, 15 December 1989.

65. John O'Reilly. Personal communication, 4 April 1990; O'Reilly slides, same date.

66. Carolyn Smyly. Personal communication, 18 December 1989; also Michael Zarb, Summer 1976.

67. C.A. O'Reilly to C.K. O'Reilly, 15 November 1884. O'Reilly Papers, BCARS.

68. Ibid. 11 June 1897.

69. Ibid. 25 May 1897.

70. C.K. O'Reilly to parents, 10 March 1897. O'Reilly Papers, BCARS.

71. Jr. Army & Navy Stores to C.K. O'Reilly, 5/12/90. O'Reilly Papers, BCARS.

72. S. Scotter to C.A. O'Reilly, 5 March 1889. O'Reilly Papers, BCARS.

73. C.K. O'Reilly to C. Hare, 11 February 1892. O'Reilly Papers, BCARS.

74. C.A. O'Reilly to Peter O'Reilly, 13 July 1888. O'Reilly Papers, BCARS.

75. C.K. O'Reilly to parents, 13 November 1896. O'Reilly Papers, BCARS.

76. Madge Hamilton, former Assistant Archivist, BCARS. Personal communication, 21 July 1987.
     Geoffrey Warren *A Stitch in Time: Victorian and Edwardian Needlework*. New York: Taplinger, 1976.
     see Chapter 8 "Tiny Fingers of the Little Child": pp. 122-136.

77. Virginia A.S. Careless. Preliminary study of the O'Keefe family, August 1988.

78. E.g., Louisa May Alcott *Little Women; Good Wives*. London: Dent (1868) 1970 p. 76.

79. C.K. O'Reilly to parents, 27 February 1885. O'Reilly Papers, BCARS.

80. Ibid. 4 August 1885.

81. C.K. O'Reilly to Peter O'Reilly, 31 December 1888. O'Reilly Papers, BCARS.

82. C.K. O'Reilly to parents, 23 March 1884. O'Reilly Papers, BCARS.

83. Ibid.

84. Ibid. 7 November 1884.

85. Ibid. 7 June 1884.

86. C.A. O'Reilly to Peter O'Reilly, 10 July 1888. O'Reilly Papers, BCARS.

87. C.K. O'Reilly to parents, 27 February 1885. O'Reilly Papers, BCARS.

88. C.A. O'Reilly to Peter O'Reilly, 13 July 1889.

89. E.g., C.A. O'Reilly to F.J. O'Reilly, 28 November 1888. O'Reilly Papers, BCARS.
     M. Bezly Thorne to J.W. Trutch, 26 February 1900. O'Reilly Papers, BCARS.

90. C.K. O'Reilly to Peter O'Reilly, 18 October 1888. O'Reilly Papers, BCARS.

91. C.K. O'Reilly to F.J. O'Reilly, 9 October 1888. O'Reilly Papers, BCARS.

92. C.A. O'Reilly to F.J. O'Reilly, 22 July 1889. O'Reilly Papers, BCARS.

93. Susan Crease Reminiscences. Crease Papers, BCARS.

94. Peter O'Reilly to C.A. O'Reilly, 29 November 1888. Pearse Collection, VCA.

95. Mrs. E. Sisson. Personal communication, 22 November 1988.

96. C.K. O'Reilly to parents, 20 August 1885. O'Reilly Papers, BCARS.

97. C.A. O'Reilly to C.K. O'Reilly, 18 August 1884. O'Reilly Papers, BCARS. A sample of Mary Augusta's hair,
     saved by her mother, is in the Pt. Ellice House collection.

98. Mrs. R. Penn. Personal communication, 17 February 1989.

99. Mrs. E. Sisson. Personal communication, 22 November 1988.

100. Ibid.

101. Peter O'Reilly to C.K. O'Reilly, 25 May 1884. O'Reilly Papers, BCARS.

102. C.K. O'Reilly to parents, 21 May 1884. O'Reilly Papers, BCARS.

103. Mrs. E. Sisson. Personal communication, 22 November 1988.

104. C.A. O'Reilly to C.K. O'Reilly, 13 September 1884. O'Reilly Papers, BCARS.

105. E.g., G. Reginald Talbot, 17 June 1945; F. Ormonde Gray, February 1885. O'Reilly Papers, BCARS.

106. E.g., Frances Cooper, 8 May 1989; Mrs. Penn, 17 February 1989; Mrs. Holmes, 22 February 1989. Personal communications.

107. Mrs. Penn. Personal communication, 17 February 1989.

108. Emily Ashley to C.A. O'Reilly, 14 October 1884. O'Reilly Papers, BCARS.

109. C. Hare to C.A. O'Reilly, 26 September 1885.

110. Peter O'Reilly to C.K. O'Reilly, 21 January 1884, 21 June 1884, 2 November 1884.
     C.K. O'Reilly to parents, 14 May 1884. O'Reilly Papers, BCARS.
     C.A. O'Reilly to C.K. O'Reilly, 2 June 1884.

111. C.K. O'Reilly to parents, 26 June 1885. O'Reilly Papers, BCARS.

112. C.A. O'Reilly to C.K. O'Reilly, 18 July 1885. O'Reilly Papers, BCARS.

113. F. Ormonde Grey to C.A. O'Reilly, February 1885. O'Reilly Papers, BCARS.

114. Agnes Murray to C.A. O'Reilly, 27 April 1885. O'Reilly Papers, BCARS.

115. C.K. O'Reilly to parents, 2 February 1897. O'Reilly Papers, BCARS.

116. Ibid. 30 October 1896.

117. C.A. O'Reilly to C.K. O'Reilly, 21 June 1884. O'Reilly Papers, BCARS.

118. The sources for the following material on activities are Kathleen's letters to her parents and brothers, as well as her parents', brothers', other relatives', and friends' MSS. The Miscellaneous files in the O'Reilly Papers at the BCARS, as well as artifacts at Pt. Ellice House also record activities. What follows in the report is a summary from these various sources, but specific references are cited.

119. C.A. O'Reilly to C.K. O'Reilly, 16 December 1896. O'Reilly Papers, BCARS.

120. C.K. O'Reilly to parents, 19 August 1884. O'Reilly Papers, BCARS.

121. Cf. E. Phillips, R.C. Harris *Letters from Windermere 1912-14*. Vancouver: UBC Press, 1984; e.g., p. 57. Cf. Dorothy Davis *A History of Shopping*, London: Routledge & Kegan Paul, 1966. Chapter 10 describes an 18th century Buckinghamshire family that shopped similarly.

122. Peter O'Reilly to C.K. O'Reilly, 25 August 1885.

123. C.K. O'Reilly to Peter O'Reilly, 4 July 1878.

124. Ibid. 13 August 1881.

125. Ibid. 16 May 1877 and c.1878.

126. Peter O'Reilly to Edgar Dewdney, 20 August 1885. O'Reilly Papers, BCARS.

127. C.A. O'Reilly to C.K. O'Reilly, 25 August 1885. O'Reilly Papers, BCARS.

128. E.g., Ibid. 15 June 1885.

129. Ibid. 25 August 1885.

130. E.g., C.K. O'Reilly, Notebooks 1882-92; 1902(-06). O'Reilly Papers, BCARS.

131. E.g., Erskine & Wall, Grocers, Victoria, B.C., 3 November 1901. O'Reilly Papers, BCARS.

132. C.K. O'Reilly to Peter O'Reilly, 26 August 1904. O'Reilly Papers, BCARS.

133. Peter O'Reilly, Diaries 1859-66. O'Reilly Papers, BCARS.

134. Margaret O.A. Ormsby "Some Irish Figures in Colonial Days" *B.C. Historical Quarterly*, 1950, XIV, #1 & 2, pp. 61-82: p. 62.

135. Charlotte Morgan-Kelly, *Trutch Family History*. Ladysmith, V.I., June 1956, p. 3. Trutch Papers, UBC Special Collections.

136. W.J. Reader *Victorian England*. London: B.T. Batsford, 1973, pp. 37, 155.

137. C.A. O'Reilly to C.K. O'Reilly, 23 February 1885. O'Reilly Papers, BCARS.

138. Jehanne Wake *Princess Louise: Queen Victoria's Unconventional Daughter*. London: Collins, 1988.
     C.J. Wake. Personal communication, Fall 1989.

139. Lorne Files. Correspondence In, O'Reilly Papers, BCARS.

140. C.A. O'Reilly to F.J. O'Reilly, 21 December 1888. O'Reilly Papers, BCARS.

141.   C.K. O'Reilly to parents, 20 June 1897; 1906, Add MSS 412, Vol. 1; O'Reilly Papers, BCARS.

142.   C.K. O'Reilly to parents, 12 July 1885; 12 November 1896. O'Reilly Papers, BCARS.

143.   W.S. Gilbert *Patience or Bunthorne's Bride*. 1881. Published in W.S. Gilbert *The Savoy Operas*. London: Macmillan, 1957. p. 204.

144.   C.K. O'Reilly to Peter O'Reilly, 13 September 1882. O'Reilly Papers, BCARS.

145.   Lou Taylor *Mourning Dress* London, 1983, p. 134.
        H.S. Stanhope to C.K. O'Reilly, 22 October 1899. O'Reilly Papers, BCARS.

146.   W.S. Gilbert *Patience*. 1881; p. 206.

147.   *The Queen*, New York, n.d., *The Ladies Bazar* Toronto, Nov. 1888; *Bazar Fashions* Toronto, April 1891. Pt.Ellice House Magazines.

148.   *The "Deluxe" Society News*. Victoria, B.C. February-April 1913. p. 8. Pt. Ellice House magazine.

149.   C.A. O'Reilly to C.K. O'Reilly, 12 February 1897. O'Reilly Papers, BCARS.

150.   C.K. O'Reilly to F.J. O'Reilly, 16 February 1892. O'Reilly Papers, BCARS.

151.   Virginia A.S. Careless. Preliminary study of O'Keefe family, August 1988

152.   Peter O'Reilly to C.K. O'Reilly, 17 August 1885. O'Reilly Papers, BCARS.

153.   C.K. O'Reilly to C. Hare, 11 February 1892. O'Reilly Papers, BCARS.

154.   C.A. O'Reilly to C.K. O'Reilly, 6 April 1897. O'Reilly Papers, BCARS.

155.   Ibid. 5 July 1884.

156.   Peter O'Reilly to C.A. O'Reilly, 10 December 1888. Pearse Collection, VCA.

157.   C.K. O'Reilly to F.J. O'Reilly, 8 April 1892. O'Reilly Papers, BCARS.

158.   Edgar Fawcett *Some Reminiscences of Old Victoria,* Toronto: William Briggs, 1912.

159.   C.A. O'Reilly to C.K. O'Reilly, 19 November 1883. O'Reilly Papers, BCARS.

160.   Ibid. 3 September 1888.

161.   Ibid. 6 April 1897.

162.   Bill, David Spencer to C.A. O'Reilly, 1 September 1898. O'Reilly Papers, BCARS.

163.   Bill, J.E. Harris to C.A. O'Reilly, 14 August 1897. O'Reilly Papers, BCARS.

164.   Ibid.

165.   See #161.

166.   See Bills, O'Reilly Papers, BCARS.

167.   Bill, David Spencer to C.K. O'Reilly, 16 April 1909. O'Reilly Papers, BCARS.

168.   RBCM catalogue card 965.561: 1907 Todd family dress.

169.   C.K. O'Reilly to parents, Christmas 1896. O'Reilly Papers, BCARS.

170.   Ibid. 29 May 1884.

171.   C.A. O'Reilly to C.K. O'Reilly, 12 March 1897. O'Reilly Papers, BCARS.

172.   C.K. O'Reilly to C. Hare, 11 February 1892. O'Reilly Papers, BCARS.

173.   C.K. O'Reilly to parents, 13 November 1896. O'Reilly Papers, BCARS.

174.   Ibid. 30 October 1896. O'Reilly Papers, BCARS.

175.   Ibid. 25 November 1896. O'Reilly Papers, BCARS.

176.   Ibid. 13 November 1896. O'Reilly Papers, BCARS.

177.   C.A. O'Reilly to C.K. O'Reilly, 23 July 1884. O'Reilly Papers, BCARS.
        Peter O'Reilly to C.K. O'Reilly, 17 August 1885. O'Reilly Papers, BCARS.

178.   Peter O'Reilly to C.K. O'Reilly, 30 August 1885. O'Reilly Papers, BCARS.

179.   C.A. O'Reilly to C.K. O'Reilly, 10 August 1884. O'Reilly Papers, BCARS.

180.   C.K. O'Reilly to parents, 23 May 1885. O'Reilly Papers, BCARS.

181.   Ibid. E.g., 3 January 1884.

182.   Mrs. R. Penn. Personal communication, 17 February 1989.

BIBLIOGRAPHY

PRIMARY SOURCES

BRITISH COLUMBIA ARCHIVES AND RECORDS SERVICE (BCARS)
Manuscript Section
Vertical File
Victoria *Daily Colonist*, Victoria *Daily Times*
O'Reilly Papers - MSS.
                Add. MSS.
Crease Papers
Archives Correspondence.

Visual Records Section

VICTORIA CITY ARCHIVES (VCA)
B.W. Pearse Collection

UNIVERSITY OF B.C. (UBC) SPECIAL COLLECTIONS
Trutch Papers

PT. ELLICE HOUSE
Magazines (see list in Appendix)
MSS.
Photographs
Catalogue, book list, files, etc.
Artifacts

ROYAL B.C. MUSEUM (RBCM)
Catalogue
Catalogue negative files
Old Catalogue Files
New Number Files
Archives records
Tags from artifacts now on exhibit
Artifacts
O'Reilly clothing collection and others.

UNIVERSITY OF GUELPH, Guelph, Ontario
Archives, Special Collections

LAURA INGALLS WILDER/ ROSE WILDER LANE MUSEUM AND HOME, Mansfield, Missouri, USA

ROSS BAY CEMETERY
O'Reilly monument

INTERVIEWS/CORRESPONDENCE

Mrs. Anketell-Jones

Canadiana Costume Society

Frances Cooper

Costume Society, London, England.

Dan Gallacher, former curator of history, RBCM

Guildhall Library, London, England.

Madge Hamilton, former archivist, BCARS

Susan Hart, Archivist, BCARS

Mrs. H.C. Holmes

Cyril Hume, period landscape consultant

Mary McMinn, former clothing and textile curator, RBCM

Inez Mitchell former archivist, BCARS

Inez O'Reilly, former owner & curator, Pt. Ellice House

John O'Reilly, former owner & curator, Pt. Ellice House

Mrs. R. Penn

Tom Palfrey, former designer, RBCM

Ivan Sayers, former curator of history, Vancouver Museum

Mrs. E. Sisson

Carolyn (Case) Smyly, former history curator, RBCM

Mary Tunnell, Costume Society member, England

Phil Ward, former conservator, RBCM

Jim Wardrop, former curator of history, RBC

Mary Witt, Costume Society member, England

Michael Zarb, former curator, Pt. Ellice House

SECONDARY SOURCES

Alcott, Louisa May · *Little Women; Good Wives.* London: Dent. (1868) 1970.

Corley-Smith, Peter · *The Ring of Time: the Story of the B.C. Provincial Museum.* Victoria, B.C.: B.C.P.M., 1985.

Costume Society of America · "New Argument Against Corsets". *Reese River Reveille,* Dec. 19, 1894, North Virginia. In C.S.A. Region V. *Newsletter,* v. 4 #2, Oct. 1988.

Davis, Dorothy · *A History of Shopping.* London: Routledge & Kegan Paul, 1966.

de Bertrand Lugrin, N. and John Hosie · *The Pioneer Women of Vancouver Island 1843-1866.* Victoria, B.C.: The Women's Canadian Club, 1928.

Fawcett, Edgar · *Some Reminiscences of Old Victoria.* Toronto: William Briggs, 1912.

Fry, Herbert · *London.* London: W.H. & Allen & Co., 1884.

Gallacher, Dan — "Exhibits as Overviews: the Case of British Columbia Modern History". in Dave Richeson, ed., *Western Canadian History: Museum Interpretations* Mercury Series #27, History Division, National Museum of Man, Ottawa, Ont. 1979.

Gilbert, W.S. — "Patience or Bunthorne's Bride." 1881. Published in *The Savoy Operas*. London: Macmillan, 1957, 2 Vols.

Ormsby, Margaret A. — "Some Irish Figures in Colonial Days." *B.C.Historical Quarterly*, v.X1V, #1 & 2, 1950:

Phillips, Elizabeth and R.Cole Harris — *Letters from Windermere 1912-14*. Vancouver University of B.C. Press, 1984. Press, pp. 61-82.1984.

Reader, W.J. — *Victorian England*. London: B.T. Batsford, 1973.

Taylor, Lou — *Mourning Dress: A Costume and Social History*. London: Allen & Unwin, 1983.

Wake, Jehanne — *Princess Louise: Queen Victoria's Unconventional Daughter*. London: Collins, 1988.

Warren, Geoffrey — *A Stitch in Time: Victorian and Edwardian Needlework.*, New York: Taplinger, 1976.

Wilson, Colleen — *Report on Operation Moth & Other Concerns at Pt.Ellice House*. Victoria, B.C.; Royal B.C. Museum, June 1988. Unpublished report.
"Moths, moths, and more moths". *Museum Roundup,* #152 B.C. Museums Association, Feb. 1990.

Zarb, Michael — *File for Pt. Ellice House Guides*, unpub. c. 1970s, Pt. Ellice House,Victoria, B.C.

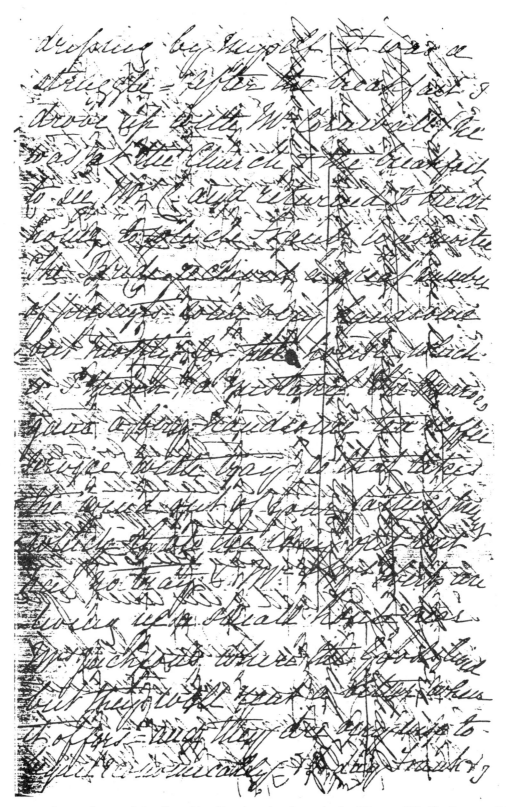

Figure 1. Page from a letter of Caroline O'Reilly, showing "crossing" of lines. O'Reilly Papers, BCARS.

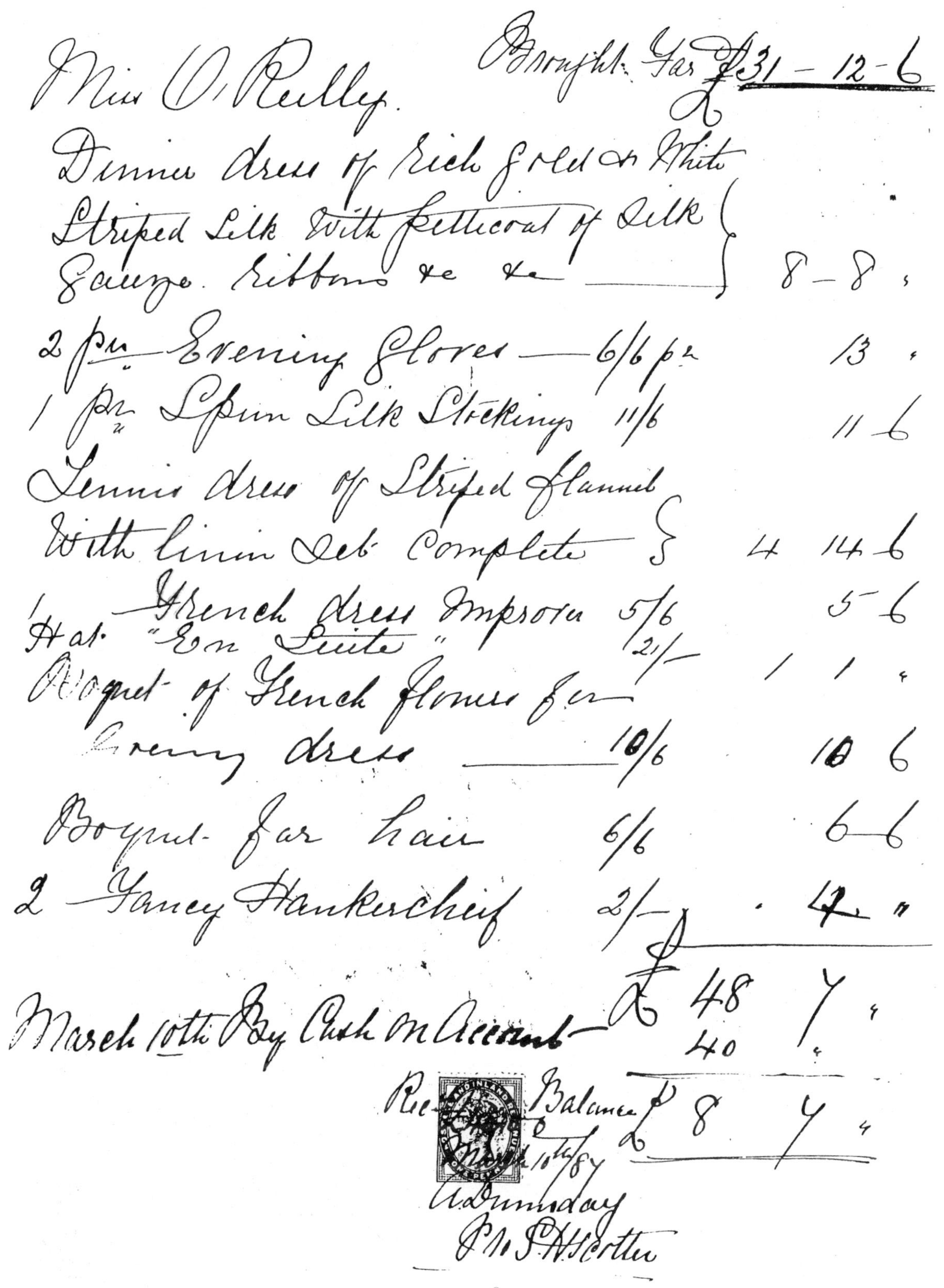

Miss O'Reilly.   Brought For £31 – 12 – 6

Dinner dress of Rich Gold & White
Striped Silk with Petticoat of Silk
Gauze. ribbons &c &c _____ }   8 – 8 ,

2 pr. Evening Gloves ____ 6/6 pr.   13 ,

1 pr. Spun Silk Stockings 11/6   11 6

Tennis dress of Striped Flannel
With linen Set Complete ____ }   4 14 6

1 Hat. French dress Imporon 5/6   5 6
"En Suite"   2/-

Bouquet of French Flowers for
Evening dress _____ 10/6   10 6

Bouquet for hair   6/6   6 6

2 Fancy Hankerchief   2/-   ·   4. "
                                    _____
                                    £ 48 Y ,
                                       40   ,

March 10th By Cash on Account ____

Rec.   Balance £ 8   Y ,
       March 10th 1887
       A Dunnday
       P M S A Scotter

Figure 2. Bill, S.A. Scotter to C.K. O'Reilly, 1887, showing detail in description. O'Reilly Papers, BCARS.

Figure 3. Kathleen O'Reilly dressed identically to sister. BCARS HP50096.

Figure 4. Mary A. O'Reilly dressed identically to sister. BCARS HP50097.

Figure 5. Laura Ingalls and sisters, 1881; N.B., Mary and Laura dressed identically. Laura Ingalls Wilder Home, Mansfield, MO.

Figure 6. Kathleen O'Reilly about three years old; N.B., dress. BCARS HP50070.

Figure 7. Child's dress. RBCM 965.1422.

Figure 8. Child's dress. Pt. Ellice House 975.1.2159.

Figure 9. Detail of photograph, Kathleen O'Reilly in tennis dress. BCARS HP50119.

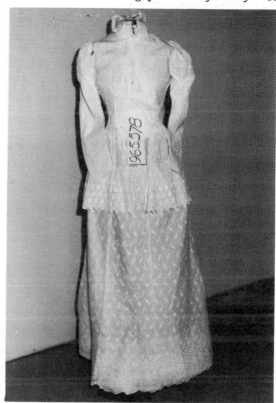

Figure 10. Kathleen O'Reilly's tennis dress. RBCM 965.578.

Figure 11 (both photos). Kathleen O'Reilly's dress, fabric the same as that in Fig. 10. RBCM 965.577.35.

Figure 12. Store advertisement; N.B., tennis dress, "Primrose". cf., Fig. 11, *The Queen*, 7 June 1890. Pt. Ellice House magazine.

Figure 13. Howell & James tea gown identified as Kathleen O'Reilly's. RBCM 965.577.22.

Figure 14. Howell & James tea gown catalogued as provenance "not established". RBCM 965.624.

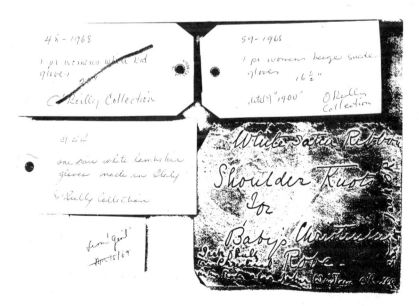

Figure 15. Tags from artifacts on exhibit, RBCM; N.B., lower right one is in Kathleen O'Reilly's handwriting.

Figure 16. Kathleen O'Reilly's bridesmaid dress, 1874. RBCM 965.1437.

Figure 17. Mary A. O'Reilly's bridesmaid dress, 1874. RBCM. 965.1434.

Figure 18. Detail of photograph, Kathleen O'Reilly at a garden party. Pt. Ellice House photograph.

Figure 19. Bodice of dress worn by Kathleen O'Reilly in Fig. 18. RBCM 965.724.

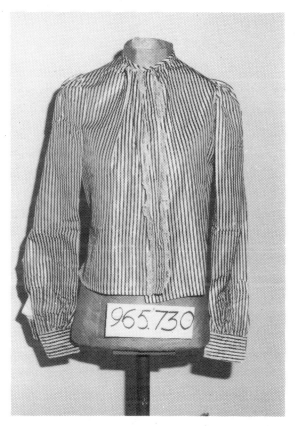

Figure 20. Kathleen O'Reilly in striped blouse. cf., Lewis Evans advertisement in Fig. 31. Pt. Ellice House photo.

Figure 21. Blouse similar to Fig. 20; N.B., has been altered. RBCM 965.730.

Figure 22. Detail of illustration from article on Second Dublin Drawing Room, Kathleen O'Reilly's presentation at Court, *Lady's Pictorial*, 27 February 1897. Pt. Ellice House magazine.

Figure 23. Kathleen O'Reilly in Presentation gown. BCARS HP19863.

Figure 24. Kathleen O'Reilly's Presentation gown;
N.B., alterations and damage. RBCM 965.577.182.

Figure 25 (below). Magazine advertisement with part
clipped out, *The Gentlewoman*, 31 January 1891.
Pt. Ellice house magazine.

Figure 26. Same advertisement as Figure 25, complete, *Lady's Pictorial*, 21 February 1891. Pt. Ellice House magazine.

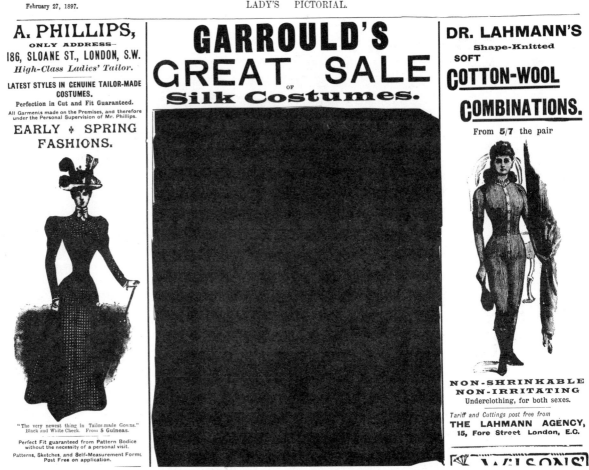

Figure 27. Magazine page with advertisement clipped out, *Lady's Pictorial*, 27 February 1897. Pt. Ellice House magazine.

Figure 28. Photocopy of clipping from Figure 27 found in letter, C.A. O'Reilly, 23 March 1897. O'Reilly Papers, BCARS.

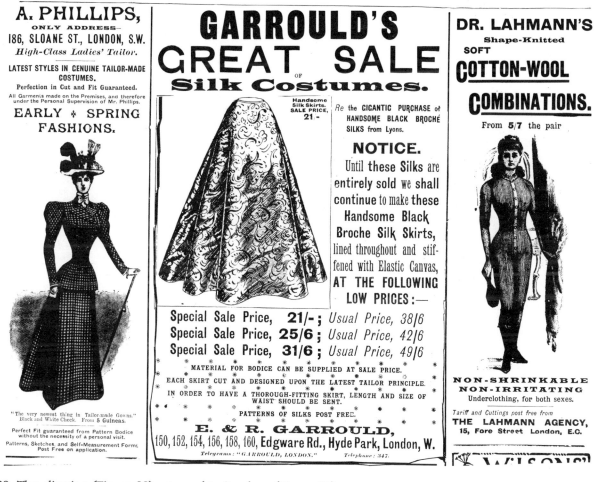

Figure 29. The clipping (Figure 28) returned to its place (Figure 27).

Figure 30. The dress made to resemble the advertisement (Figure 28). RBCM 965.577.23.

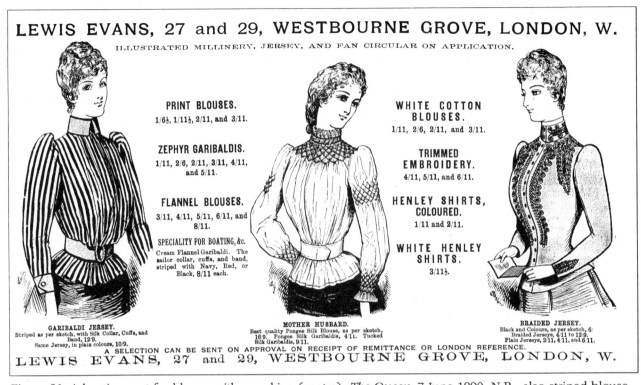

Figure 31. Advertisement for blouse with smocking (centre), *The Queen*, 7 June 1890; N.B., also striped blouse, cf., Figures 20 and 21. Pt. Ellice House magazine.

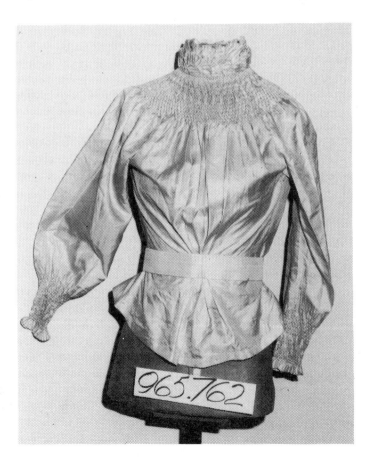

Figure 32. Blouse resembling advertisement in Figure 31. RBCM 965.762.

Figure 33. Advertisement for Cording's, mentioned in Kathleen O'Reilly's notebook. *The Queen*, 7 June 1890. Pt. Ellice House magazine.

Figure 34. Bodice catalogued as provenance "not established", bearing the label of Caroline O'Reilly's dressmaker; N.B., trim. RBCM 965.766.

Figure 35. Skirt piece with same trim as Figure 34; an identified O'Reilly artifact. RBCM 971.60.94.

Figure 36. Bodice inside showing crude
alteration; N.B., coarse stitching in dark
thread, dart and sleeve lining seams open.
RBCM 965.577.36.

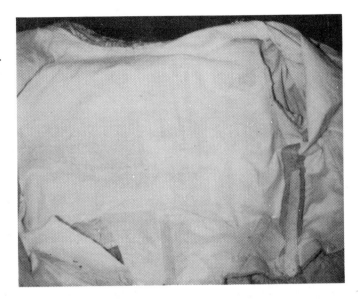

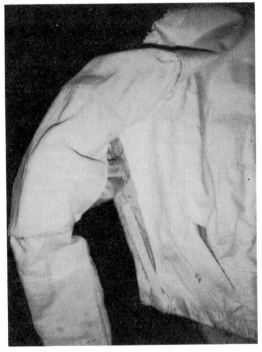

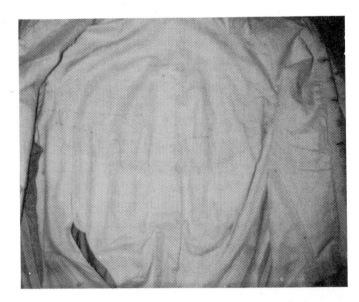

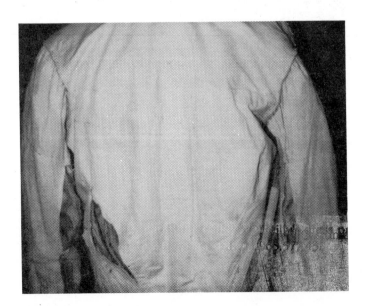

Figure 37. Dress outside, piecing in neck and yoke does not show at a distance. RBCM 965.577.36.

Figure 38 (below). Magazine illustration; N.B., similarity of #3734-3733 to Figure 37. *The Ladies' Home Journal*, June 1908. Pt. Ellice House magazine.

3808-3385   3736-3737   3734-3733   3883-3746   3478-3555

Figure 40 (right). Kathleen O'Reilly's dress bodice disassembled. cf., Kathleen wearing the dress, Figure 42. RBCM 965.577.43.

Figure 39 (below). O'Reilly dress showing alteration in progress; N.B., neck edges opened and turned under, skirt section pinned to bodice. RBCM 965.577.26.

Figure 41. Kathleen O'Reilly's dress prior to disassembling. RBCM 965.577.43.

Figure 42. Kathleen O'Reilly in dress in Figures 39 and 40. BCARS HP50078.

New Argument Against Corsets

This
is the
shape of
a woman's waist
on which a corset tight
is laced. The ribs deformed
by being squeezed, press
on the lungs till they're
diseased. The heart
is jammed and
the liver
is a
tor-
pid lump;
the stomach
crushed, cannot
digest; and in a mess
are all compressed. Therefore, this silly woman grows to
be a beautiful mass of woes,
but thinks she has a lovely
shape, though hideous
as a crippled ape;

———

This is
a woman's
natural waist,
which corset never
yet disgraced. Inside it
is a mine of health. Outside,
of charms it has a wealth,
It is a thing of beauty
true, and a sweet joy
forever new. It
needs no artful
padding vile
or bustle big to
give it "style"
It's stong and solid,
plumb and sound, and
hard to get one arm
around. Alas! If women
only knew the mischief that
these corsets do, they'd let
Dame Nature have her
way, and never try her
waist to "stay."

from the Reese River Reveile, Dec. 19, 1894,
Austin, NV. *Submitted by Jan Loverin*

Figure 43. Graphic representation of the evils of tight lacing, and a more desirable alternative. Costume Society of America, Region V Newsletter, v. 4 #2, October 1988:5.

Figure 44. Kathleen O'Reilly (first woman on left) as a bridesmaid in Nellie Ward's wedding, Victoria, B.C., 1898. BCARS HP99303.

Figure 45. Detail of bird's-eye view map of part of London, England, 1884 showing streets where Kathleen shopped, especially New Bond Street and Clifford Street (location of dressmaker, Scotter). Area close to clubs, St. James' Palace, Pall Mall. Herbert Fry *London*. London: W.H. Allan & Co., 1884.

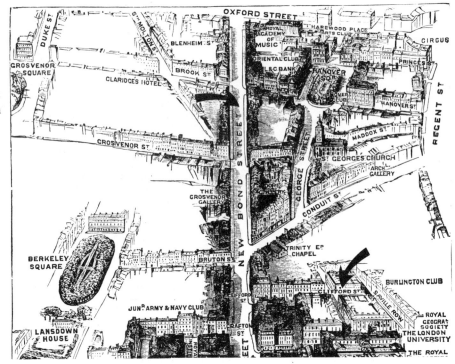

Figure 46. Magazine advertisement for Hotel Metropole, patronized by the O'Reillys when in London, England. *The Queen*, 17 May 1890. Pt. Ellice House magazine.

DICKINS & JONES.

NEW FASHION BOOK, full of charming Illustrations, sent free on application.

"ETINCELLE."

A very handsome and original ball-gown of yellow gros royale silk, veiled with draperies of white net closely embroidered with crystal shaded amber beads, the effect of which by gaslight is extremely brilliant. The skirt is trimmed with a long trail of yellow roses, a spray of the same lovely flowers being placed on the bodice. The back draperies are formed of full folds of net, with a deep hem embroidered with amber beads. In front the net draperies are drawn down and held in place by straps and rosette bows of yellow ribbon, arranged in the manner shown in the sketch. The bodice is of yellow silk, with epaulette bows of ribbon. Price, including Bodice (unmade), 8 Guineas. Floral Garniture, 18/9 extra.

Russian Net Ball Dresses in all Colours, on satin foundation, 58s. 6d. (bodice unmade).

A Choice Variety of Floral Garnitures, from 18/9 to 52/6 the full Set.
Can be sent on approval.

DICKINS AND JONES, 232 to 236, Regent-st., W.

Figure 47. Magazine advertisement for dress. *The Queen*, 18 January 1890. Pt. Ellice house magazine.

DICKINS & JONES

THE LILY.

It is of white satin draped entirely with a fine quality net, and having a deep ruche round the hem, which is sprinkled with sprays of lilies of the valley. The low-cut bodice is of white satin, also draped with the net, and the short sleeves are of net edged with a fringe of the lilies. Round the basque tying in a bow on the left hip, and terminating in long ends knotted with lilies, is a wide band of white satin ribbon, and the whole effect is girlishly sweet and simple.

Price for Skirt and Trimmings for Bodice, 78s. 6d.; also on Batiste foundation, 68s.

DICKINS & JONES, REGENT ST., LONDON.

Figure 48. Magazine advertisement for dress. *The Queen*, 13 December 1890. Pt. Ellice House magazine.

Figure 49. O'Reilly dress resembling Figures 47 and 48. N.B. dress has two bodices; the one without flowers was left in the process of being altered: the sleeves are missing and the satin trim is detached in places. RBCM 965.577.30.

Figure 50. Magazine advertisement for tea gowns, Howell & James, London, England. cf., Figures 13 and 14. *The Queen*, 7 June 1890. Pt. Ellice House magazine.

Figure 51. Kathleen O'Reilly wearing a tea gown. cf., Figures 13, 14 and 50. BCARS HP50163.

(2898——2899)

Fi;ure 17.—Ladies' Toilette.

Figure 52. Magazine illustration of a dress, *The Ladies Bazar*, November 1888. Pt. Ellice House magazine.

Figure 53. Kathleen O'Reilly wearing a dress similar to Figure 52. BCARS HP50086.

Figure 54. "New and fashionable styles of hairdressing sketched at Mr Jean Stehr's, 235 Oxford Street", London. *The Queen*, 13 December 1890. Pt. Ellice House magazine.

Figure 55. Kathleen O'Reilly with hairstyle similar to Figure 54. BCARS HP87413.

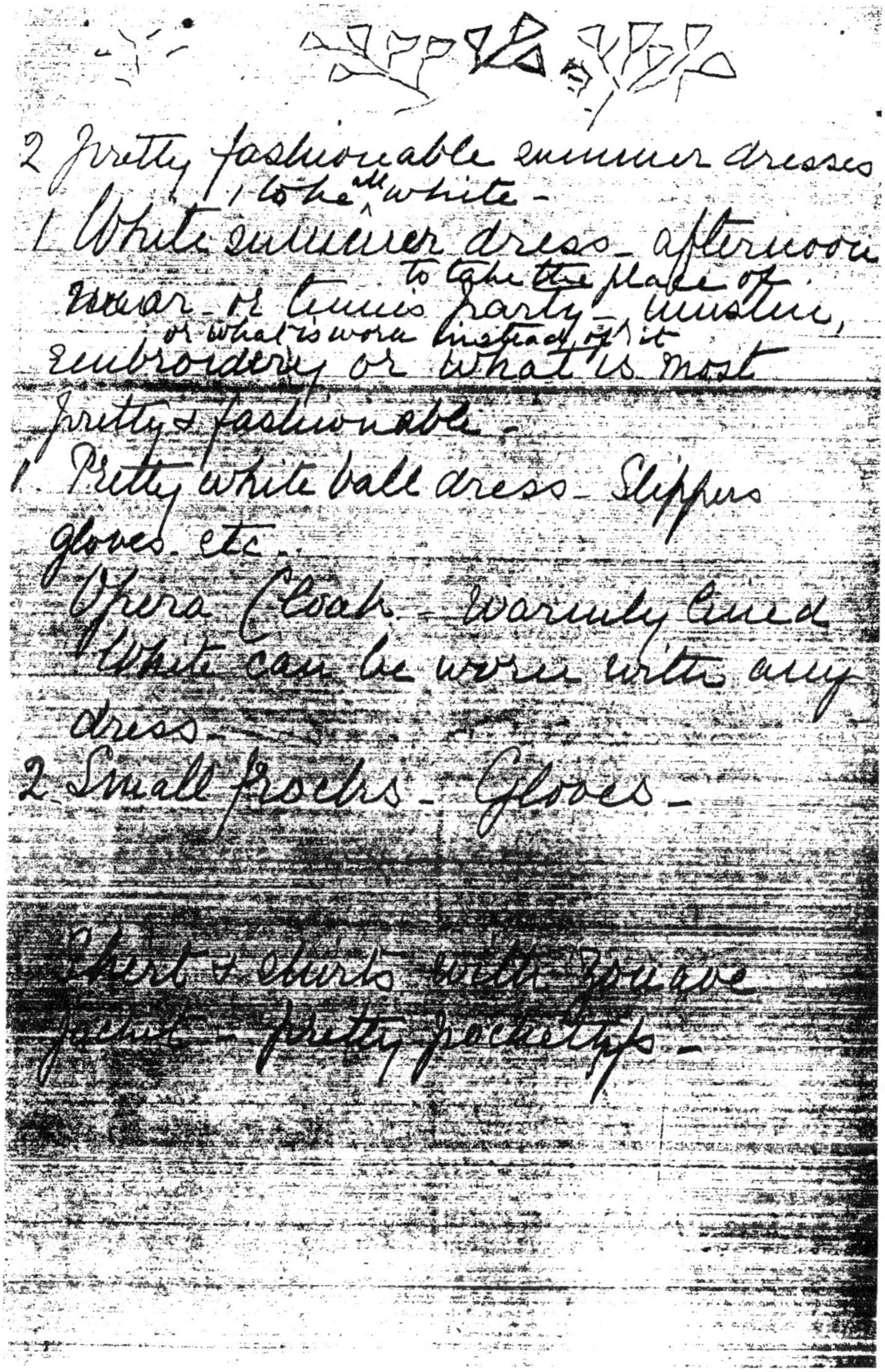
2 pretty fashionable summer dresses
1 to be white -
1 White summer dress - afternoon
to take the place of
wear - or tennis party - muslin,
or what is worn instead of it
Embroidery or what is most
pretty & fashionable -
1. Pretty white ball dress - Slippers
gloves etc -
Opera Cloak - warmly lined
White can be worn with any
dress -
2 Small frocks - Gloves -

Skirt & shirts with Zouave
Jacket - pretty pockets -

Figure 56. List of clothing requested, Kathleen O'Reilly's handwriting; N.B., mention of "pretty, fashionable". O'Reilly Papers, BCARS.

Figure 57. Photograph of Englishwoman; N.B. hairstyle, dress. *Lady's Pictorial*, 21 February 1891.Pt. Ellice House magazine.

Figure 58. Kathleen O'Reilly in hair style, dress resembling Figure 57. BCARS HP50079.

Figure 59. Magazine illustration; N.B., dress on right. *The Queen*, Christmas 1911. P. Ellice house magazine.

Figure 60. Magazine advertisement, Shoolbred's, London, England; N.B., pose of model. *Lady's Pictorial*, October 1912. Pt. Ellice House magazine.

Figure 61. Kathleen O'Reilly in dress and pose resembling Figures 59 and 60. cf., Figures 40 and 41: this dress at RBCM. BCARS HP50078.

Figure 62. Kathleen O'Reilly, N.B., hat. BCARS HP50082.

Figure 63. The Crease daughters and friends, Victoria, B.C.; N.B., hats. BCARS HP 22935.

Figure 64. Kathleen O'Reilly as a child, 1876. BCARS HP50003.

Figure 65. Detail of photograph: Laura Ingalls as a child. cf., Figure 64: dress and hair style, neck detail and decoration. Laura Ingalls Wilder Home, Mansfield, MO.

Figure 66. Kathleen O'Reilly; N.B., hat, bodice, gloves, pose. Pt. Ellice House photograph.

Figure 67. Lucy Maud Montgomery c. 1898. cf., Figure 66. The L.M. Montgomery Collection, University of Guelph Library.

Notes